BRITISH TANGANYIKA

ROBERT HEUSSLER

British Tanganyika

An Essay and Documents on
District Administration

Durham, N. C.
Duke University Press
1971

PRINTED IN THE UNITED STATES OF AMERICA
BY HERITAGE PRINTERS, INC.

To the Future of Trenton State College

ACKNOWLEDGMENTS

For necessary financial help I wish to thank the American Philosophical Society, the Social Science Research Council, and the University of Vermont. Deep appreciation goes also to Dame Margery Perham, Professors P. J. Bohannan, L. Gray Cowan, and W. B. Hamilton and A. H. M. Kirk-Greene for letters of recommendation.

It is a pleasure to have this opportunity of recording my gratitude to the President of Tanzania, Dr. Nyerere, and to Vice President Kawawa for kindly granting me permission to examine materials in rural administrative headquarters and in the National Archives.

J. J. Tawney and I. Lloyd Phillips of the Colonial Records Project, Oxford, gave vital help in assembling the impressive Tanganyika collections of that project, in guiding one's use of these, and, in Mr. Tawney's case, in introducing me to a large number of retired Tanganyikans. Mr. Tawney also criticized the first draft, as did two other former members of the Tanganyika service, Dr. A. Sillery of the Taylorian Institution and E. G. Rowe, supervisor of the Commonwealth Services Course. Blessed is the student of history who receives knowledgeable, hard-hitting comment before publication.

I am grateful to University College, Dar es Salaam, for a research associateship and to F. W. Deakin and P. C. Hailey, warden and bursar respectively of St. Antony's College, Oxford, for senior common room membership and for use of college facilities.

For research and logistical help of many kinds I thank Dean F. G. Burke of the State University of New York at Buffalo, L. B. Frewer, superintendent of Rhodes House Library, Oxford, Professor Norman N. Miller of Michigan State University, M. G. Cook, director of National Archives, Tanzania, B. Cheeseman, librarian of the former Colonial Office Library, and Professor S. K. Bailey of Syracuse University.

The maps were prepared by Margaret M. Kane, with the advice of Professor H. G. Barnum, Department of Geography, University of Vermont.

I am endebted to the following people for a wide variety of contributions, mostly in the form of written or verbal advice on the particulars of district administration, viewed from professional or scholarly standpoints: D. A. Anderson, W. S. G. Barnes, H. C. Baxter, P. L. Birkett, the late R. Bone, D. N. M. Bryceson, J. C. Chande, H. N. Chittick, J. S. R. Cole, M. J. Davies, B. J. Dudbridge, Sir John Fletcher-Cooke, W. A. Forbes, H. A. Fosbrooke, P. P. Gawthorne, O. Guise Williams, P. H. D. Haile, R. Haszard, L. M. Heaney, J. F. R. Hill, A. B. Hodgson, H. Holdsworth, J. B. Hooper, A. H. Jamal, S. A. Kandoro, A. Y. A. Karimjee, Z. E. Kingdon, A. B. P. Kirrita, P. A. Kisumo, F. J. Lake, E. A. Leakey, D. F. B. LeBreton, F. LeDuc, A. Lenzner, J. A. K. Leslie, R. M. Leslie, W. W. Lewis-Jones, J. M. Liston, F.

Longland, I. F. C. Macpherson, H. H. Magnay, R. A. J. Maguire, Professor M. M. Mahood, R. S. W. Malcolm, F. P. S. Malika, C. M. M. Masanja, G. M. S. Mawalla, H. H. McCleery, Dr. K. J. McCracken, M. J. B. Molohan, the late Dr. Eduardo Mondlane, A. B. Moore, S. Mshoti, B. Mulokozi, E. S. K. Mziray, M. J. S. Newman, D. S. O'Callaghan, A. A. Oldaker, W. F. Page, F. H. Page-Jones, R. Pentney, Professor R. C. Pratt, Mrs. H. Rayne, J. Rooke Johnston, Mrs. G. Russ, S. J. Saidi, B. W. Savory, J. P. Singano, Professor R. F. Stephens, Sir Rex Surridge, B. Sutherland, W. B. Tripe, R. W. Varian, Sir E. Vasey, S. A. Walden, W. Wenban-Smith, Miss J. Wicken, G. M. Wilson, W. Wood, F. H. Woodrow, and Dr. R. Yeager.

Finally and very importantly I offer thanks to the wives and families of many of the above for their hospitality and for valuable embellishments on male remembrances of times past in Tanganyika.

CONTENTS

CONTENTS

GLOSSARY AND ABBREVIATIONS

The meaning of certain Swahili, Arabic, and tribal words has been given in footnotes to particular sections such as the Savory safari diary. The following words appear with some frequency in the text and also in the documents. I thank Dr. A. Sillery for providing translations which have in mind both literal meanings and common usage.

Akida: Government agent or headman under the German system, continued by the British in some areas, their functions being determined by the wishes of administrative officers and by the circumstances of local societies.

Askari: Soldier or policeman.

Baraza: Public meeting; place of meeting; veranda.

Boma: Fort; administrative headquarters.

Bwana: Master.

Duka: Shop.

Fitina: Intrigue.

Fundi: Artisan; skilled workman.

Jumbe: Village headman.

Liwali: Fairly senior Arab official or magistrate.

Mndewa (pl. wandewa): Chief, e.g., of the Wadoe.

Mwami: Chief, e.g., in Bukoba or Uganda.

Safari: Journey; tour of inspection.

Shamba: Farm; garden; plantation.

Shauri: Plan; advice; discussion; affair, e.g., matter that eventuates in a legal complaint.

Waziri: Chief officer of state under a monarch.

N.B. Tribal groups are referred to variously in the text, either with the prefix *Wa* (the Watongwe) or without it (the Tongwe).

DO - District officer

ADO - Assistant district officer

PC - Provincial commissioner
NA - Native authority
NT - Native treasury
KAR - King's African Rifles

A - National Archives of Tanzania
CRP - Colonial Records Project of Oxford University

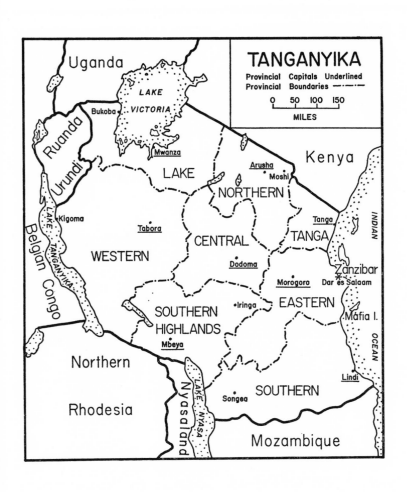

TANGANYIKA

Provincial Capitals Underlined
Provincial Boundaries ▬ ▪ ▬ ▪ ▬

0   50 100 150
MILES

Uganda

LAKE
VICTORIA

Bukoba

Mwanza

Ruanda
Urundi

Kenya

LAKE

NORTHERN

Arusha
Moshi

Kigoma

LAKE TANGANYIKA

Belgian
Congo

Tabora

WESTERN

CENTRAL

Dodoma

TANGA

Tanga

INDIAN

Morogoro

Dar es Salaam

Zanzibar

Iringa

EASTERN

Mafia I.

SOUTHERN
HIGHLANDS

Mbeya

OCEAN

Northern

Lindi

Nyasaland

LAKE NYASA

Songea

SOUTHERN

Rhodesia

Mozambique

BRITISH TANGANYIKA

CHAPTER ONE

Introduction

There is a growing scholarly interest these days in the historical role of Europeans in other parts of the world. Some of the new work builds on that section of modern history that concerns the expansion of Europe, beginning usually with the age of exploration and culminating in the scramble of the 1880s and 1890s. Other studies proceed backward, as it were, from the still continuing era of nationalism, being motivated in part by a wish to inquire into the immediate colonial background of independence movements since 1945.[1] Whatever their starting point or particular outlook, researches into imperialism are to be welcomed as contributions to an understanding of the whole great historical complex that we call European civilization, both domestically and farther afield.[2]

Tanganyika's[3] imperial experience came very late in the day. Germany did not bring the territory under full administration until around the turn of the century. The devastation of the 1914 war made it necessary for the British to rebuild, in some areas virtually from the ground up. Their rule lasted less than half a century, an unusually short period by imperial standards. Nonetheless, it may be asked, for purposes of perspective, how the Tanganyika case compares and what its particular characteristics were. This is best approached perhaps by first inquiring whether imperialisms have a typology of their own, separate enough from that of metropolitan governments to allow them to be considered as a distinct political species. Is imperialism a valid subject, a coherent specialty within history?

---

1. A recent work of great importance in the field is Philip Mason's *Patterns of Dominance* (London, 1970).

2. Cf. W. H. McNeill, *The Rise of the West* (Chicago, 1963), in which all of modern history is seen in this context of European culture.

3. The name of the country was changed in 1964 to Tanzania, but the old name will be used throughout, for historical reasons and to avoid confusion.

It does not appear to be so except insofar as interracial confrontation gives all imperialisms a common theme. No matter how different they were in place and time they all did involve some measure of rule by men of one race over people of another. That aside, each seems essentially unique, made up of indigenous and imported materials that produce in the aggregate a spectacle and experience that were *sui generis*. The Spaniards in Middle America stayed a very long time, exploited the natives, fought among themselves over the aims of their imperium and the rights of the Indians, and evolved a hybrid society that eventually replaced the purely Iberian government and ended by stamping most of the area with a Hispanic-American culture that still survives. In India the early British went to trade, stayed to administer, and never really thought it possible to make the place English. There was a certain amount of mixing but on nothing like the Spanish-American scale. The inheriting elites were British in much of their governmental ethos and language, but European religions, pure or diluted, did not make much progress, and the people as a whole, while more united politically and commercially than their seventeenth-century forebears, remain today overwhelmingly Indian in culture. Imperialism in nineteenth- and early twentieth-century China was fragmented. It never quite succeeded in taking over the whole place. While it was enormously destructive of domestic unity and self-confidence, its challenges finally hardened native resolve to turn away from the country's outmoded glories and to beat the Europeans at their own game. And French imperialism in West Africa followed a still different course. There was some talk, as in the Spanish case, of bringing the natives to the font of Europeanism, but neither proselytism nor miscegenation reached the proportions of Spain's in Mexico. There was a certain affectation and artificiality to French rule, in that much of it started in a purely military way and did not enrich the metropole commercially nearly as much as Britain's in India had done. The result was neither rabid xenophobia as in China nor the creation of a large mestizo elite, virtually divorced from the rest of society and defining social success in unabashedly European terms, as Latin American Creoles had long done in their rather pathetic and forlorn way. The present-day West African concern with evolving a home-based and retrospective literature has no counterpart in former Spanish or Portuguese America.

Different as they have been, it is possible to ask of all imperialisms the same kinds of questions. What sort of people were the imperialists? That is, what occupational, educational, and social backgrounds did they come from? What were their motivations and, if different, the real and ostensible explanations put forward by their sponsors? How strong were they in numbers, military power, and finance? What were their relations with the metropole? What cultural state did they find the natives in at the time of contact? Was there considerable unity among local peoples or not? Were they wealthy or not, and were they spread out widely or confined to a fairly compact area with efficient communications? As time went on what relations developed? Was the alien control absolute or was its posture more derived, with natives continuing to perform most of the political tasks? Was there large-scale commercial exploitation? What influence was exercised by the aliens over education and religion? How long did the imperium last and how amenable to change did both parties prove to be? Which culture, alien or indigenous, made more concessions to the other? Was the end of foreign dominion violent or peaceful, and after independence was there a continuation of alien influence in another guise?

The need for close, precise monographs addressed to such questions will be obvious, for without them we generalize from insufficient evidence. If this is true for specialists it is that much more so for writers of textbooks and other works of wide scope. Because it concerns exotic parts of the world, imperialism has been less intimately known to such writers than have the main streams of European and North American history or the high cultures of Asia. In the absence of a flourishing and familiar literature it has been only natural that they would occasionally fall back on a kind of moralistic impressionism that can end in caricature.[4]

Tanganyika at this writing still lacks a definitive history. Monographic material on both the precolonial and the colonial periods is sparse. The aim of this short book is to characterize district administration in the British years, from the end of World War I until the early fifties, when Tanganyika stood, though no one knew it, on the

4. See, for example, the citations on imperialism in Crane Brinton, John B. Christopher, and Robert Lee Wolff, *Modern Civilization* (Englewood Cliffs, N.J., 1957), a much used text, and in Arnold Schrier et al., eds., *Modern European Civilization* (Chicago, 1963), a book of readings.

threshold of self-government. The fragment is offered as a minor contribution, a brick for the wall, in the thought that the full-scale history that will someday be undertaken might benefit from this and similar studies of particular aspects of European rule.

The focus in these pages is on district officers (DOs) and their work.[5] In the first years of British rule, up to 1925, the territory was divided into some two dozen districts with a DO in charge of each, and they all reported directly to the capital in Dar es Salaam. In the nature of things, as will be seen, the authority and autonomy of DOs was very considerable, in some cases virtually absolute. Later, with the creation of provinces, some of the DOs' functions were supervised and coordinated by the way-station of provincial headquarters, which added more bureaucracy but seldom reduced local discretion. In essence DOs were the kingpins, doing much of the work personally and having a hand, one way or another, in everything that took place in their districts—tribal administration, agriculture, commerce, education, animal husbandry, communications. The unfolding story of the country's development involved many people whose work could be reckoned as important as the DOs'—teachers, agriculturalists, governors in times of innovation and large expenditure of outside funds—but perhaps they themselves, in the aggregate, had the best overall view of events and the closest personal involvement year by year.

At the time of one's wanderings in Tanganyika districts and of formal research, there and in England—the early fifties to 1968—several former officers were encountered whose service dated from 1914 and a great many who worked in the country at one time or another from the twenties to independence. Talks were held with serving officers in their bomas (district headquarters) or on safari, with others in Dar es Salaam and provincial headquarters, and with still others in England and the Channel Islands after their retirement. A goodly number have presented diaries and personal papers to the Colonial Records Project of Oxford University, including J. J. Tawney, director of the project and himself a Tanganyika administrator with twenty years of service. More papers have come from relatives of deceased officers. Official materials consulted in Tanganyika include administrative and other correspondence, both

5. The title district officer was changed in 1940 to district commissioner, but to avoid confusion DO will be used throughout the present work.

Secretariat and provincial, and district books still kept in bomas as of the sixties.

In line with the questions on imperialism mentioned above, I have been concerned in this book to ask who the first political officers were, what social conditions they found as they took over their districts during the 1914 war, how they proceeded to establish themselves, and what initial administrative tactics were used and why. What were the reactions of the British and the Africans to each other? What changes took place as time went on, and what overall characterization may be made of British rule in its core period? While it may be permissible to add a tentative word about effects, it should go without saying that an appraisal of Britain's net impression on Tanganyika would be premature at this time. It is in any case the Africans themselves, and students of African history, who will undertake this when the time comes.

CHAPTER TWO

Starting Out

The early officers were a mixed bag. Growing up in the West Country and when he was at Beaumont, F. J. E. Bagshawe thought of being a veterinary surgeon. Animals and the open countryside were his idea of a happy and interesting life. But his father, a judge by profession and a man of moderate means, considered that sort of doctoring less than gentlemanly. Young Frank and his cousin Arthur went out to Africa to raise horses instead. O. Guise Williams, with even less money behind him, dreamed of going to Canada to farm. When a chance came to take a job as assistant manager of a cattle ranch in Rhodesia he saw it as the answer to his boyhood ambition. He would save money for Canada. It was not long after his arrival in Africa in 1906, however, that all thoughts of any other place wafted away on the winds, and the soil and people and languages of Africa had taken possession of him. The big continent worked its wiles on E. H. A. Leakey and W. F. Page too. Leakey's father, a Devon farmer, told him there was no money in agriculture in Edwardian England. The alternative, teaching school, did not appeal. But planting coffee in Kenya was something else—a whole new life in a country where one's home-grown skills counted for more than they did in Exeter and where, with luck, a comparable risk offered higher rewards. Page, though his social background was different from Leakey's and included a Public School education, had somewhat the same outlook. To farm in Central Africa was to taste adventure and at the same time to lay the foundations of a successful career. And F. Longland well remembers that English boys growing up at the turn of the century saw Africa as a kind of wild west. They thrived on tales of Livingstone and Stanley, Emin Pasha and Richard Burton. His circle knew George Grenfell, who was working in the Congo before the Belgian government took over. Longland had been training for a career in civil engineering and a job as station engineer with a missionary group near Stanleyville offered a chance to combine his professional knowledge with excitement beyond the farthest hopes of any London draftsman. In 1907 when he arrived the Eastern Congo was living its red rubber days.

All over Africa before 1914 such men, with their counterparts from Germany, Portugal, France, and elsewhere in Europe were going their separate ways, thinking their own thoughts and mingling their lives, each in his own fashion, with the Africa of the moment. They were Europeans still. But Europeans with a difference; not cut off from home but removed from it and spiritually apart from those who had stayed behind. Many would spend most of their lives in Europe and only twenty to thirty years in Africa. But those would be the best years and they would mark a man, leaving him for ever different from other people in some subtle way.

When they ran across their fellow Europeans in Africa on the other hand, British expatriates often felt that they had more in common with them than with their own countrymen back home. Africa somehow bound them together and muffled the nationalism of Europe. One's relationship to the African was not an after-hours thing, and other white men, regardless of national origin or job, were socially congenial.[1] At times it was not entirely unlike medieval society with its wide-ranging class ties and its relatively well-defined local divisions between the agricultural mass and those above them. Then came 1914. Overnight one's affinity to the home country became paramount again. Some like Page went back to Europe to fight their war there. Many stayed in Africa and were joined in local campaigns by young compatriots coming out for the first time.

For Longland the resumption of Englishness was delayed a bit. Being in Belgian territory when war broke out, he was commissioned a sous lieutenant in the Congo forces and advanced with them against the nearest Germans in Ruanda-Urundi and later all the way to Mahenge in the south central part of German East Africa. Guise Williams enlisted as a rifleman in the First Regiment, Rhodesian Army, which helped to crush the Boer Revolt and then went against German Southwest Africa. These were still the lackadaisical days

1. In the words of a former DO, "the stark fact was that in earlier days there was a complete absence of cultural and social affinities," i.e., with the Africans. J. J. Tawney, letter of 4 October 1968.

of time enlistments, and in 1915 the regiment was mustered out. The choice was to go to France or to German East Africa, the last remaining enemy-held territory in that part of the world. Guise Williams chose the latter for two reasons: everyone assumed the show in France would not last long, and East Africa might be a place to try one's luck in after the fighting was over. His first unit was the Northern Rhodesia Rifles, but soon, because he knew Chinyanga, he was put in charge of six hundred porters who accompanied some police troops preparing to attack the Germans across the border from Abercorn. Guise Williams's work as they moved into the southern highlands and around the tip of Lake Nyasa was mainly intelligence, mixed with fighting whenever an enemy force was engaged. He was wounded in 1917 and sent to hospital in Songea. Here there would be yet another change of unit. As soon as he was fit he took a lieutenant's commission in the King's African Rifles. By now it was late in 1917.

W. S. G. Barnes, the son of an Indian army officer, found himself in England when the war started. He saw an advertisement put out by the Legion of Frontiersmen calling for men who could ride and shoot. After signing on, he discovered that action would await a six-month training period, so he transferred to the East African Mounted Rifles, who were just sailing for Kenya. The unit, whose composition and conditions of service were somewhat vague, proved on arrival in Nairobi to be almost completely settler-dominated, its commissions reserved for public school men. Barnes was assigned as a trooper in Squadron A ("Monica's Own," named rather grandly for the governor's daughter). He began service as an intelligence scout. Based at Voi, he spent the first two years reconnoitering German positions, sometimes alone, sometimes with one or two African soldiers.

For them all political work was a logical extension of soldiering. In 1917 the new British military administration asked for Longland, then at Kigoma, because he knew the country and could manage languages. An assistant political officer in the British service at that point did much the same things as a lieutenant in the Belgian Army did, and there was a certain logic in being with one's own people now that most of the country was safely in Allied hands. Barnes landed in military administration as a consequence of illness. At Voi he came down with a bad case of fever and was given leave in England to recover. On return he was better but still not up to active service. In May 1917 he joined General O'Grady's column moving inland from Lindi and was given political work because that was something a man only half well could do and because everyone in good physical condition was needed at the front. The sense of this, undeniable at the time, was to dog the reputation of Tanganyika for many years afterward and cause it to be said, quite unfairly, that the whole of the early political service were merely soldiers manqué. Physical incapacity was certainly a factor in Guise Williams's case. He was recovering from wounds in a South African hospital when a letter came asking if he would accept immediate appointment to the political service. But with more than a decade of African experience behind him, including a year in German East, he was a reasonable choice, especially in view of what would be demanded of the first officers. In December 1917 he accepted the lowest administrative rank—subassistant political officer—and started for his post. The route was through Portuguese East Africa, then by paddle steamer on the Zambesi and a Lake Nyasa boat to Mbamba Bay. From there he walked a hundred miles to Mahenge and reported to Capt. A. H. L. Wyatt.

What officers did during the first years varied from district to district and depended upon the way they applied their interests and abilities to situations they found on arrival. Longland's first post was at the old mission station of Urambo Kilimani (Urambo on the hill), some fifty miles northwest of Tabora. He was alone. Under ideal conditions a runner from Tabora could reach him in two days, but it took a week for news of the Armistice to come through. No one knew enough to feel confident that the war in Europe would end favorably, nor would anyone be so rash as to predict that the much respected German commander in East Africa, Lettow, was finished once and for all. It was not even certain exactly where he was. At Urambo Longland showed the flag by being there and did what he could to run an incipient administration. Tax was collected in German coin. When he wrote—infrequently—to his superior in Tabora he did so on the backs of German letterheads still lying about. There was no other paper. An epidemic of flu was raging at the time, which made him a doctor, though a rather puzzled one who wondered why quinine had no effect. Most officers did a certain amount of road building and repairing from the start. At

Mahenge Wyatt concentrated on this and left the cash book to Guise Williams, who also handed out seed so that a beginning could be made in attacking the famine that war had left behind. Along the Ruvuma Barnes would be occupied with boundary disputes and getting Portuguese cooperation in dealing with tax evaders and kidnappers of women. Everywhere one tried by any available means to build confidence throughout a country that understandably saw the white man as a bringer of violence and disruption.

Until they found out who was who among the local people, officers could not really come to grips. In some places there was no doubt. Sheikh Rama, liwali of Bagamoyo, conducted himself during the British assault and capture of the port in such a way as to make clear that he had the qualities of a leader: self-respect, ability, courage, the confidence and support of the community.[2] The first British officers ashore found him directing the work of putting out fires started by the bombardment, and he soon proved himself as valuable to the new rulers as he had been to the Germans. Elsewhere Lettow had taken local officials and middlemen away with him as he fell back, leaving tribal chaos behind. Barnes held a baraza at Tunduru in January 1918 in an effort to learn which of the various claimants to power were recognized by the people.[3] Each man who had asserted a claim was made to stand in front of the crowd, and those who accepted him as their leader were told to queue up behind him. Bagshawe was doing the same thing in Kondoa.[4] If such tactics were not completely foolproof, they were found to be basically reliable in most places, for tribesmen would not usually misrepresent themselves in public.

Nevertheless, intimidation was always a possibility, and any additional check was welcome. In some parts German records were captured intact or were traced and dug up. German certificates of appointment to various tribal or administrative offices were produced by Africans on the assumption that the new white men would govern in the same way as the defeated ones had done. And indeed

2. Interview, Rooke Johnston, 20 January 1965; cf. Bagamoyo District Book.

3. Interview, Barnes, 13 January 1965; Barnes also bluffed missionaries at Masasi into revealing the whereabouts of buried German records.

4. See Bagshawe diaries, 23 February 1920, CRP.

if the British with their small staff had been able to reassemble the German machinery of local government pretty much as it had been they would have considered themselves fortunate. The old system, for all its special characteristics, shared one essential with British structures in other parts of Africa: it fitted into and adapted itself to indigenous forms in each locality and exerted pressure on those forms according to the balance of their strength in relation to its own.[5] Along the coasts from Lindi to Tanga tribal hegemony had been watered down long before the Germans came. Generations of Arabs and other newcomers had traded with local peoples, ruled them, and intermarried with them, producing various hybrid Swahili communities not unlike the Macanese of the South China coasts or the Goanese in India. The long-term effect was naturally to atomize indigenous groups and give intermediate and high-level authority to others—first the Swahilis and their Arab masters, then the Germans, who employed Swahili intermediaries roughly as their predecessors had done since Portuguese times. The Maji Maji Rebellion, an African revolt in the first decade of the twentieth century, was put down by the Germans with great bloodshed, and this further weakened tribal groups in back of the coasts and brought about a coincident increase in the power of Swahili overrule. Elsewhere African invaders had succeeded in imposing their rule on native tribes and in gradually carving out little empires for themselves, these being treated with deference by the Germans if the power of the African units had survived Maji Maji and other challenges. It made just as much sense to use paramount chiefs on the shores of Lake Victoria and Lake Nyasa as it did to employ tried and true akidas and liwalis on the coasts. One was facing realities and accommodating to them.[6]

At Mahenge a single akida remained behind after the German withdrawal, and he went on under Wyatt, his functions virtually unchanged. In supervising tax collections the akida dealt directly with a large number of petty village chiefs or pastoral leaders who called

5. Interview, Longland, 2 February 1965; Singida and Kasulu were military districts, with garrisons, in the German time. Nevertheless some strong chiefs survived in a number of areas because there were not enough German officers or akidas to maintain full administration.

6. Cf. Arusha District Book, entries in the period 1929 to 1933.

themselves sultani, although they were in effect no more than elected headmen of their communities. C. J. Bagenal, who had charge of Tabora from the middle of 1917 on, learned from German documents which chiefs and akidas were recognized by his predecessors and what their functions had been. On the basis of this information together with his own investigations he confirmed or refused the claimants who presented themselves in all of the surrounding area. On his own initiative Bagenal also gave to each recognized local authority, with some ceremony, a "book" defining their rights and duties. This simple document outlined the procedures to be followed in native courts and the types of cases that the holder of the book was empowered to hear, such as petty theft, drunkenness, and matrimonial and property disputes. At Kigoma, where he took over from the Belgians in 1921, the same procedure was gone through again, and as before the basis of it all was German documentation in the office and German certificates of authority brought forward by chiefs and lesser native officials.[7]

Although they would make departures from German methods very soon and although in toto their own system differed markedly from the German, the first district officers were conscious of a substantial debt to the departed enemy. The physical inheritance alone—everything from buildings to railways to the research station at Amani—was considerable. Beyond this there was the long-established habit of European discipline and the large corps of trained underlings ready, willing, and able to continue it at the bidding of new masters. More than one early British officer became aware of the enormous initial advantage that was his as a consequence of Allied victory in the war. If the Germans had been regarded as supermen in their former colony, the conquerors of supermen must be that much more awesome and miraculous. In any event the victory had been won against a gallant, resourceful, and respected foe. As the 1920s began there was little residue of enmity between the new rulers and those Germans, mainly missionaries and settlers, who stayed behind or returned from Europe. At Bagamoyo the DO, Major H. Rayne, received the thanks of the German community for having their monument in front of the boma

7. See Turnbull at Mwanza to land officer, Dar es Salaam, 25 April 1922, on the German legacy in the Lake Victoria area and especially on the "Kiwanja" system, A.

repaired, and F. W. Bampfylde, a later DO, assigned a station hand to keep the German cemetery clean.[8]

With the war over and the new territory, now called Tanganyika, divided into districts, the officers in charge got down to the daily round. A place hummed or ticked over or stagnated according to the abilities of the man who was posted to it.[9] There was also the uniqueness of each district and subdistrict, the special qualities of weather, terrain, communications, and native life that surrounded the best officers and the worst with particular limitations or opportunities.

At Kigoma and Ujiji in the early twenties, remembers Longland,

There was no daily stint (of a regular kind) . . . how could there be? Who knew what would turn up? The door of the boma was open all day and sometimes at night a native would knock you up about some matter . . . a man being killed by a lion or a woman murdered by her lover. You might get a white hunter concerned with arms licences and game laws. An Indian trader might come in asking about opening a new store. When you went on tour these things had to wait until you returned. There was something to do all the time and . . . your duties did not depend upon routine but on how hard you were prepared to work.

There might be a European or South African policeman on the station, or a stock inspector. More often one was alone. There was no telephone, no telegraph, no wireless. Communication with headquarters, or with your next door neighbor, was by native runner and very slow. Living conditions were very primitive. No one ever heard of ice or a refrigerator . . . no electric light, no mosquito-proof buildings, and sanitary conditions [were those] of the early middle ages. There was no doctor.

Malaria was common and dangers lurked in the bush. Two D.O.s were killed by elephants and one by a buffalo. Nine people of my acquaintance committed suicide, three of them District Officers. There was a certain amount of strain working in tropical Africa.[10]

8. See District Book, 1931 to 1940.
9. Some DOs "didn't care twopence." Longland notes, 29 April 1965.
10. Letter, 23 May 1965. Much later, at Arusha, a major boma, Longland and Rooke Johnston locked the door and went off for days at a stretch. Government was so much dependent on the district officer that when he was

DOs knew that nine-tenths of native life went on as always behind their backs and without reference to them. An officer learned what was going on when chiefs and others called on him at the boma or when he himself went out on safari. Longland was able to report a murder to Dar es Salaam on one occasion only because two chiefs casually mentioned to him the circumstances in which they had had to kill one of their female relatives. When a chief died, especially an important one, there was an opportunity to learn a lot, for if he had the energy and inclination a DO could oversee the whole process of succession. It happened that way twenty miles from Songea when Longland was first there. He walked out to the late chief's village by one route and back by another, holding big and little barazas on the way. At the village itself there was "a big, informal walla walla about everything," the DO sitting by as a general assessor.[11] When the talk stopped he gave them his own summation and then put proposals to the elders.

Though he delighted in this sort of thing and spent a good deal of time working out a free and easy relationship with the people, Longland's special passion was designing, mapping, and all the practical jobs of engineering that lay open to DOs with an interest in them.[12] The Germans had done the best they could with mapping, but many of their early charts were drawn in Berlin by professionals who had never seen the country. "Maps showed tracks which perished years ago and gave the names of villages deserted long since. Hills were deduced where there were none . . . rivers were made to run the wrong way."[13]

Therefore when Dar es Salaam decreed that the colony's local ordinances and laws could not be enforced until boundaries had been accurately defined, "the wretched district officer was almost at his wits' end."[14] Boundary disputes between tribal groupings were inherited from the previous administration and many went right on for years in the British period. It was especially difficult in areas that lacked natural limits (the vast majority), and so one

---

not present the actuality of administration was gone and only the aura remained.

11. Longland notes, 29 April 1965.

12. He eventually wrote a book on field engineering which the government issued as a guide for the use of administrative and other officers.

13. Letter, 4 October 1965.

14. Ibid.

spent weeks and months on safari with plane table and compass, pacing off endless local dividing lines after endless barazas where competing claims of the chicken and egg kind stretched back farther than the memory of anyone alive. Someone had to decide, and the DO did. Though the elders on either side would always grumble, "the legal bigwigs appeared to be happy, the local peasants did not care a hoot and the D.O. passed on to his next fence."[15]

In some places the war heritage of disruption and violence was still to be contended with and a basis laid for the condition of un-questioned obedience that later officers would come to take for granted. Along the road in Masasi, Barnes had to maintain order with a small contingent of police. Seeing to it that the road stayed open and doing the necessary maintenance was an irksome busi-ness of conscripting local labor and keeping men at work who were unaccustomed to regular hours or to discipline of any kind. Occa-sionally his own superiors made the task harder by issuing orders without having enough knowledge of what the carrying out of these would mean in the districts. Barnes refused to compel women to work on the road, not out of humanitarian promptings but because the presence of women would have completely disrupted the work of male gangs nearby.[16] There were incidents that showed the need for improvement in relations between civil and military branches of the new government. On one occasion a troop of King's African Rifles (KAR) had made off with some women in Barnes's area and had then been intercepted by the DO's police. When Barnes arrived on the scene the confrontation between the two units was at boiling point and the African sergeant in charge of the KAR was defiant when Barnes ordered him to turn the women over. With the KAR's white officers hunting game a few miles behind, the situation was critical. The DO ordered his own NCO, a corporal, to place the sergeant under arrest, which he instantly did. The tension, tem-porarily relaxed, immediately resumed however when the KAR officers appeared a few moments later and demanded the release of their sergeant. The DO met this challenge by threatening to send off a report to Lindi that the KAR had misbehaved when deserted by their officers. Barnes offered a compromise that would let the

15. Ibid.
16. Barnes was overruled by his superior on this issue but stuck to his guns and was finally backed by General O'Grady, then in command at Lindi.

KAR officers save face: if they would move out forthwith and promise to court-martial the sergeant, he would release the man and consider the incident closed. This worked. Although he never found out whether the other part of the bargain was kept, he had the satisfaction of showing in public that the DO was responsible for order in his district and that he was capable of enforcing his authority even in the face of superior arms.

Farther north in Kondoa and later in Moshi and Iringa, Bagshawe spent most of his time on foot safari.[17] The boredom of long walks in the bush was relieved by shooting lions and other game and by being all things in all situations as they came up. He doctored himself and another DO for fever, the constant companion of everyone on tour. He set a broken leg of a village woman in the Gogo country and treated a man whose jaw had been half torn away by a lion. In Kondoa his principle interest was bringing more system and planning into the work of farmers: ". . . launched my 'agriculture for profit' scheme. If it comes off it will revolutionise the district. If it doesn't, Lord knows where we shall finish."[18] And through tax collecting and court work he slowly brought more order to local administration. By appointing akidas and assigning tribesmen to certain headman and chiefs he laid the groundwork for accountability and regularity, where before there had been a tangle of competition and constant movement from one area to another. Even the nomadic and untamable Masai were fined—in cattle—for fighting with their neighbors or decamping to new pasture lands without permission.

When commenting on colleagues and juniors Bagshawe gave a picture of his own values and general outlook in pages that are otherwise singularly free of abstractions about the job. With a young New Zealander who had come straight into administration from military service he felt a sympathy and a bond of common experience—"he can't grasp that war and warriors have ceased to be the all in all. I suffered from the same complaint myself."[19] Hard workers won his approval always. Keenness and willingness to learn by trial and error made him forgive an unsure young sub-

17. Bagshawe was often out of touch with the boma long enough to lose track of the date, and he had to guess at it when he wrote in his diary at nightfall. See Bagshawe diaries, CRP, especially entries in the volumes covering 1917 to 1921.
18. Ibid., 25 October 1921.
19. Ibid., 10 September 1919.

ordinate for being the son of a peer. But the line between soldiers and johnnys-come-lately who had not been in the war was drawn from the start.

He was bitter about the government's failure to employ an ex-officer "who knows and likes the country and the natives, who speaks the languages and could step right into the work," while at the same time he thought the Colonial Office was bent on filling every opening with "the waste of the universities."[20] And he spoke for bush DOs everywhere in "straffing" higher authority for loading him up with "gup" and demanding reports on nonsensical subjects when he had serious work to do. The job was the thing—bringing peace and prosperity to a ravaged countryside. What Tanganyika needed was strong men who worked hard. Bureaucracy was a nuisance and an irrelevance.

As time went on officers grew more interested in tribal organization and more knowledgeable about what could be expected of the various native leaders. Kazigo bin Nkilagwamva, a chief in Shinyanga District, was described by one DO as "weak, unintelligent and quite lacking in any sense of responsibility to his people."[21] Another thought him greatly improved and felt that although he was not a strong leader he should receive sympathetic understanding in view of the known difficulties of ruling a heterogeneous area.[22] And a later officer disagreed with all of his predecessors, finding the chief "upright . . . well liked and respected by his people."[23]

The disagreements reflected not only the individual tastes of officers but also what they wanted chiefs to be and do. To some the position of a chief in his tribe was not a thing that Europeans need worry about as long as the man could be depended on not to cause trouble and to help with projects such as planting cotton or clearing bush tracts to reduce the destructive effect of tsetse flies. But others worked instinctively to refashion African structures in the direction of European local government. The mere presence of the British and the demands they placed on chiefs, akidas, and others tended to have this effect. A headman who was denied the

---

20. Ibid., 1 February 1920 and 1 January 1918, respectively.
21. Turnbull, senior commissioner in Mwanza, 9 August 1922, Mwanza District Book. And see the comments of Bell, ibid., 14 September 1922.
22. Ibid., McMahon, DO Shinyanga, 18 March 1924.
23. Ibid., Scupham, 20 January 1925.

right to make war on his neighbor in the traditional style and who took part in tax collection and road building became that much less African and more European. Whether or not the whole process was surrounded with elaborate rules and statements of intent, the chiefs and lesser native officials were formally subsumed under the colonial administration in the usual way, with the governor confirming new tribal heads when they succeeded to power.[24] Soon DOs, though they would talk about respecting tradition, were judging chiefs' performance by standards that gave more to Europe than to Africa with every passing year. Chief Gabriel Ruhumbika in the Lake Victoria area, wrote A. M. D. Turnbull, "was most attentive in assisting the Government and in giving effect to instructions . . . for the improvement . . . of the Chiefdom,"[25] and at Dodoma, H. Hignell, who was famous for opposing changes in native life, nonetheless tended to follow Rousseau in favoring compulsion when it brought greater freedom and prosperity. He made tax defaulters do road work, built a rest camp and distributed pigs to farmers even though they appeared suspicious and reluctant to take them.[26]

The days of laissez-faire were gone with the war. Everyone, even the reticent Gogo and the primitive people of remote Ufipa, come to accept the pattern and pace of life under British rule. The economy regained and then surpassed its prewar levels. Missions expanded their educational work. Asian traders and white settlers went about their business in ways that would have been familiar to colonial officials in the West Indies, Malaya, or Ceylon. A new territory had joined the far-flung, disparate collection that was Britain's colonial empire, and now it would move with the others through a stable period of development and growing self-consciousness. In no two districts of Tanganyika would the rhythm of tradition and change be quite the same. Nevertheless there would be a common theme of interaction between European and native values and ways of doing things. People in high places would speak about this, and attempts would be made to control it. Yet throughout the remaining time before war came again, DOs would observe that change was essen-

24. Byatt came to Mwanza in 1923 for this purpose, after the normal investigations of administrative officers into tribal genealogy. See the Mwanza District Book, entries by Wyatt, Turnbull, Guise Williams, and MacGillivray.
25. Mwanza District Book, 1925.
26. Hignell to chief secretary, 13 February 1922, A.

tially a matter of natural selection. They could keep the peace and use native authority (NA) tax money differently than the Africans would have done if left to themselves. But their numbers would remain small. And the horizon of opportunity open to the country's own people would widen faster than ever before in its history.

CHAPTER THREE

The Many Worlds
of the District Officer

If there had been a typical district in British Tanganyika and a typical district officer the historian's job would be simple indeed. In fact diversity was the rule. Conditions varied enormously from place to place and over time, and no two administrators were alike. Drawing a character sketch of district life becomes therefore a matter of finding major themes and putting them in with bold strokes, then adding a certain amount of detail and hoping that the end product will be representative. It would be hard to imagine an exercise that more heavily confirmed the historical axiom about uniqueness in human affairs and about differences being more pronounced than similarities. People with orderly minds and a liking for neatness and regularity in real life will find the subject an affront to their most basic sensibilities. And those who bemoan what they see as an increasing regimentation throughout the world are likely to smile with nostalgia at the stubborn individuality of local affairs in Tanganyika during the British years.

Each situation did have the same categories of determinants, the same set of bottles as it were, although the wine varied a lot. Every district, including those close by the colonial capital, had primitive communications and was governed by an administration with incomparably less money to spend than was available to governments in more advanced countries. Everywhere the force of native tradition was a counterbalance to European initiative, whether that force was a positive thing, drawing inspiration and energy from its own values and ways, or a passive phenomenon, born of apathy or cultural weakness. There were natural factors such as soil and rainfall. And behind each DO's personal makeup there was the factor of the central government's system and policy, the degree to which it helped or hindered him, left him alone or placed demands on him that took up his time and shortened the hours he could spend on other things.

Lack of money meant a small staff. During the average interwar year there were some 150 to 170 administrative officers in the territory, including men on leave or otherwise unavailable for district postings. No matter what they wanted to do on their own initiative or what headquarters instructed them to do, there were never enough men for the task.[1] It was a common experience, even as late as the 1930s or later, for junior officers to find that they were the first white men to visit remote parts of their districts.[2] In 1937 a provincial commissioner (PC) noted the effect of staff shortages in his province: "We are, I fear, doing little more than marking time and getting done the work that comes to us without . . . attempting any progressive administration."[3]

Matters improved somewhat after the 1929 depression but sank to a new low during the ensuing war, when some districts had to do without European officers altogether for extended periods.[4] And even with full-time officers on duty in some of the smaller districts the hand of government could be weakened by poor communications. In Lindi Province in the mid-twenties a junior officer whose leave time had arrived turned over his district to a cadet and started walking down the road toward the coast some two hundred miles away.[5] When he had gone forty miles or so a native runner met him with a message in a forked stick—"don't turn over." As the runner was from headquarters at Lindi the DO ordered his column of three dozen porters to pack up, and they all marched back to Tunduru, where he sent a message to the coast asking for clarifica-

1. See for example Bagshawe, PC Southern Highlands Province, to DOs, 16 February 1926, A, complaining of insufficient attention to the governor's new native administration policy, and 12 November 1926, drawing attention to the need for economic crops.

2. Savory notes, 17 March 1965, on Kasulu. And cf. DO Njombe to PC, 10 July 1929, A.

3. Partridge to chief secretary, written from Dodoma, 29 June 1937. Cf. the remarks of his predecessor, Hignell, to chief secretary, 17 January 1935, A, on discontinuity of staff.

4. Cheyne, PC Eastern Province, to DOs, e.g., to DO Bagamoyo, 4 January 1941, A, on the necessity of the liwali taking over such duties as judicial work, leaving much of the rest for administrative officers to look into on safari.

5. Interview, Page-Jones, 7 January 1965.

tion. Two weeks later he received the curt answer—"come ahead." But when he eventually reached Lindi six weeks after having first started no one knew anything about his case.

Wastefulness of this kind was offset by advantages. Remote DOs, cut off from their superior for long stretches, were close to their people in ways that made government seem a tangible and beneficial thing, approachable, sympathetic, and effective.[6] But all in all, scarcity of staff and slow, undependable communications acted as a brake on what government could do. Strict and close accountability of rural officers to the central government was seldom a possibility.

Native conservatism, another factor of great importance, took many forms. Superstition, inherent everywhere, was so complex a social force that officers sometimes thought themselves too ignorant to oppose it in particular cases.[7] A Kasulu DO who defied the ancient taboo against giving burial to chiefs was warned against the course he had decided on, not only by natives, who confidently predicted dire consequences, but also by one of the White Fathers, a future bishop.[8] The priest naturally favored Christian burial for the dead chief. But he knew from long residence in the country that patience and compromise were usually the better part of valor. Of greater importance was a massive imperviousness to change, an instinctive keeping to traditional ways that was as natural as it was frustrating to progressive administrators. Tanganyika officers found, as did their opposite numbers all over European Africa, that alien notions of educating the young were often resisted. In some places boys had to be dragooned into schools, and they knew they could count on the support of their elders if they subsequently escaped.[9] It was the same with European ideas of good government. Chiefs and their councils were the bane of DOs' existence, as will be seen,

6. Tawney, MS, Buha, 1940s, p. 24.

7. On witchcraft I have benefited from the comments of R. W. Varian and A. Sillery.

8. Tawney, MS, p. 40, and Rooke Johnston, MS, Kigoma, 1930s, pp. 16–17.

9. DO Mwanza to DO Shanwa, 1 November 1929 ff., A, on getting boys back to Mwanza Town School, e.g., Pazi bin Juma who ran away and was reportedly given refuge by Subchief Kapongo of Nassa. Cf. Whybrow diaries, 1926–1928, Ussoke, CRP. Education was eagerly sought elsewhere however, e.g., in Chaggaland.

in resisting or failing to respond to European suggestions and projects designed to improve the lot of the people. Thirty years after the start of British administration in Arusha, by no means the most backward area in the country, an officer had to admit defeat on an animal husbandry problem because the indicated solution was "out of the question politically," that is, the chiefs and elders would not see the sense and cooperate.[10]

When they tried to do anything that would require a raising of purely local horizons DOs came up against an extreme parochialism that was well nigh universal in the territory. As the capacity of government increased, officers naturally thought of moving populations out of areas that were uneconomic, especially since empty land was plentiful and house construction was both cheap and simple.[11] More often than not such moves were fiercely resisted, and plans were frequently dropped when it was seen that tribal dissatisfaction would heavily outweigh any possible economic improvement. Localism was not always unwholesome. When a smallpox epidemic struck Dar es Salaam District in 1929 the idea of fleeing the area never occurred to the people, and the DO was therefore able to put a vaccination program into operation without fear of the disease spreading.[12] Many officers in fact saw the provincialism of their people as an immutable thing that it was better to work with than against. Nevertheless native blindness or opposition to progress was hard for Europeans to accept. The Ndorobo and the Masai must be made to see the value of forests to water conservation and therefore to cattle, the economic center of their universe.[13] Overburdening pasture tracts in Maswa and Kwimba, similarly, would exhaust the land and bring famine and must be stopped, along with destructive farming methods.[14] Rules were made and DOs saw that NAs enforced

10. DO Arusha, Troup, to PC, 4 November 1947, A. A year later the same DO had to report that local councils, which the secretary of state for the colonies had recommended, were not possible because the people would neither understand nor cooperate with so abstract a notion and plan. See also Troup to PC, 30 July 1948, A.

11. ADO Liwali District to PC Lindi, 22 January 1935, A. And see Monduli District Book on the reluctance of Masai elders to let boys from Loliondo go to Monduli to school; entries of 1944 by Page-Jones.

12. Interview, Baxter, 4 April 1965.

13. Monduli District Book, Baxter, 24 February 1933.

14. DOs' conference, Lake Province, minutes, 15 September 1945; Mitchell, acting PC Arusha, to DO Mbulu, 17 May 1927 ff., A.

them: "Every owner of a paddock is hereby ordered to protect the soil from erosion caused by the grazing of cattle."[15]

European and African tendencies aside, natural factors could be the most compelling determinant of all. A PC in Dodoma saw the prevention of soil erosion as the key to everything in his province.[16] Cotton growing in the Lake Province eventually became a factor that tended to humble everything else, and tsetse in Shinyanga produced such pressure on the land that political rearrangement was a need that the most conservative chief could be made to see.[17]

Such were the main facts of life, the coordinates of the situation into which every officer stepped, regardless of his background and personality. What the coordinates added up to was an extraordinary opportunity, if he would seize it, for the administrator to exercise personal discretion.[18] In very few governments elsewhere in the world, then or since, has there been greater scope for men to make their own mark in their own way. The country was so big, there were so few men on the ground, and there was so hopelessly much to do that one almost had to choose certain activities and give them priority over others. Inevitably these would be the things that officers were particularly interested in, their hobbies or areas of special competence. The situation and the system meshed in such a way as to make DO individuality the rule, even though provincial officers thought of themselves as loyal to the government and considered that their reactions were in no basic way at variance with its wishes. Perhaps the most important determinant of administrative effectiveness in each district situation therefore was the sum total of the DO's attributes and inclinations. In the nature of things there were saints and sinners, laissez-faire types and bulls in the china shop, respecters of circulars from headquarters and men who went their own way, soldiers and scholars, middle-aged men and young men. There were endless variations in intelligence, imagination, and

15. Molohan, DO Mbulu, 20 June 1938, A.

16. Handing-over notes, Partridge to Hartnoll, 12 December 1939, A.

17. McMahon, Shinyanga, Mwanza District Book, entry describing certain voluntary Sukuma combinings in 1925; see also Medical File 404/H regarding the effect of sleeping sickness on population movements and the economy in Kiberege, 1939–1940, A.

18. A former DO observes, however, that "one was always a prisoner to some extent not only of the past but of the environment" and that government policy, though loosely applied, "did keep people pretty well on the same road." E. G. Rowe, personal communication, 7 February 1969.

health, and in that indefinable quality that helps one man to get along well with the natives and keeps another from doing so. Some liked bush life and could stand the loneliness. Others were not cut out for it. A failure to reconcile one's own psyche with the brute realities of life would drive some to the same refuge of alcohol that has long been sought by people with similar problems everywhere in the world. A few would go a bit queer. One officer of the earlier period used to fly his own personal "house flag" from the boma. He had his boys serve him dinner in the back of an old car that no longer ran and sometimes they pushed him about the station in it. In the 1940s when a DO and his wife called on their opposite numbers in a neighboring district they found the other couple living in a dreamworld of enchanted mountains and animals with magic powers. Marital problems that might have been resolved in less exotic surroundings caused a likable and respected DO to shoot himself. Most former officers looked back on their Tanganyika service with gratification and with pleasurable thoughts. But strains were severe and leave time was a vital respite in which to look on a different society and remind oneself that the African way, with all its madness and all its charm, was not the only way.

The relationship between the DO and the people of his district was partly a matter of routine and partly of projects that he pursued on his own. A unifier in the whole amalgam was the DO's function of broker between competing cultures, sometimes necessitating a forcing of the issue by him, more often requiring him to judge and give instructions with respect to conflicts as they arose. The clash was bound to be especially noticeable in an area as precise as law, with its unspoken yet universally accepted prescriptions on the native side and the written codes that Europeans invariably produce on theirs.[19] With nearly a decade of rural experience behind him Bagshawe was well aware that native law called for compensation rather than fines or imprisonment in cases of personal injury and that a man's family could pay if he was unable to do so himself.[20]

19. A clear distinction must be made between native law and custom, which NA courts dealt with, under DO supervision, and colonial law, which was codified and was binding on DOs in their magisterial capacities. DOs could do a lot to influence interpretation and, ultimately, decisions in native courts. In their own courts and dealing with the High Court they were far more circumscribed.

20. Bagshawe, PC Southern Highlands, to DO Tukuyu, 29 November 1927

Yet the law stood fast on personal accountability, which was incomprehensible to the people and correspondingly hard to enforce. The officer's preference was to defer to custom while exercising a gentle but firm supervision that would gradually change that custom in the direction of European views. In this, however, he was sometimes overruled by the High Court. On one occasion a DO's decision was reversed on a legal technicality, causing a third-time offender to be released from custody. When a similar decision by the High Court let a murderer off in another case the effect was more serious.[21] Native opinion in the district concerned had been strongly on the side of the DO who had caught the culprit, and the court's action brought British justice into disrepute, leaving the local officer with a residue of confusion and dissatisfaction to deal with.[22] At times the legal authorities in Dar es Salaam seemed to inhabit a different ideological universe from the local administrator and his people. A puzzled DO recalls:

> Early in my time at Kasulu I sentenced some cattle thieves to 18 months. Anxious that the case should contain nothing likely to cause the judgement to be upset by the High Court, I looked for a precedent and found an identical case taken by my predecessor who, in giving judgement, drew attention to the dangers caused by the crime and the worry of law-abiding people. These reasons, he said, caused him unhesitatingly to pass the stiffest sentence open to him. The case came back from the High Court with the sentence confirmed, the reviewing judge commenting that, although on occasions it would be wrong to take local circumstances into consideration, in this case he sympathized with the Magistrate's views which he regarded as sufficient justification

---

and 27 February 1928 to chief secretary; and DO Tukuyu to PC, 27 April 1928, 30 October 1928; acting chief secretary to PC, 31 December 1928, and PC to DO Tukuyu, 13 January 1931, A.

21. Interview, Page, 7 April 1965.

22. Interview, Varian, 13 January 1965. In this interview there was discussion of a popular protest that forced the attorney general to reverse himself in the case of a paramount chief in the Western Province who had taken the estate of a man who died without heirs; cf. E. C. "Jumbe" Baker, Musoma: "European influence did much to decrease the popular acceptance of the tribal code." Extracts from District Books, National Museum, Dar es Salaam, no date. Baker was in Musoma from 1924 to 1927 and in 1931. He was later PC Lake.

for the sentence. The case was identical with my own and I copied the judgement out word for word and confidently sent off my case to Dar es Salaam.

Many days afterwards the case file arrived back, with the sentence heavily reduced on the grounds that it had been wrong for my judgement to be swayed by local circumstances. The judge who confirmed the sentence given by my predecessor and reduced mine was one and the same. I wrote respectfully to the High Court, sending them both cases and asking how could such a thing be? There was a long pause. Then the judge, a man who afterwards became Chief Justice in the Gold Coast and who was exceedingly popular with Administrative Officers for his sympathy and understanding, replied. While agreeing, he said, that both cases appeared identical, it also appeared that on one occasion he had made up his mind one way and on the other he had made it up differently.[23]

But a majority of cases were managed informally at the local level without respect to the outside world. When a chief in the Western Province wanted to break the power of a witch doctor both the PC and the DO were with him as a matter of course, but they disagreed on how best to deal with the matter.[24] The chief had ordered his people to burn their fetishes and to drink water that would free them from the witch doctor's spell. They drank the water and threw their fetishes, small wooden figures with holes in them for spirits to enter and leave by, in a pile outside the village. But they balked at setting fire to the pile. Feeling ran high. The two British officers were faced with an emotional situation that involved them whether they liked it or not, for the community naturally waited to see what they would do. In a small way European civilization was on trial, confronted directly and openly by the pretensions of a force that they could only regard as irrational and repugnant. The DO, very much a no-nonsense type, wanted to burn the pile of fetishes himself and so demonstrate the superior power of the government's law. But to the PC it was enough that he and the DO openly back the chief in what had already been done. The witch doctor's influence would then fall of its own weight. This was the

23. Tawney, MS, p. 25.
24. Interview, Longland, 2 February 1965.

course that was taken, and in a few days the PC's moderation was rewarded as the people returned to their normal pursuits, leaving their chief in possession of the field.

To the average DO the heart of the matter was reconciling customary and British law by simplifying the procedures so that the ordinary native could understand. This was an issue that everyone could agree on in principle—the Colonial Office in London, the Tanganyika Secretariat, and the provincial administration.[25] It was widely known that difficulties existed, such as the impracticability of getting testimony if a native had to walk a long distance to act as a witness. Most natives could not be expected to grasp so abstract and alien a notion as the law of evidence or the concept of being innocent until proven guilty. More latitude was needed so that DOs could get at the facts in particular cases. Offenders would usually admit their guilt in the relaxed atmosphere of the village and at the time the crime was committed. But this was inadmissible by European standards, and it was not long before natives learned to keep silent and later deny their guilt in court. If the aim was "simpler law and better justice" then native convenience and custom would have to be made the basis of it all.[26] Most DOs would have sympathized with the annoyed outburst of a junior officer in the 1930s: "make the punishment fit the crime and the law be damned."[27] And most of them quietly made their own compromises ad hoc. J. Rooke Johnston looked over the voluminous papers of a murder case in Kigoma and could make nothing of them. He got a friend in the police to send him from another district an African employee with a talent for detective work. The man came to the DO ostensibly as a personal servant. After several days of listening to gossip in the marketplace he was able to supply Rooke Johnston with everything he needed to understand the case, and after a conviction was obtained evidence poured in to confirm it heavily. The High Court reversed this on technical grounds, but the DO's typically empirical solution showed the people who was boss and demonstrated that

25. In 1932 the Secretariat sent a circular to PCs advising them that the Colonial Office would soon send out a commission to look into criminal justice from the standpoint of native needs. PCs asked for DO comment. See the comments of W. F. Page, DO in the Lake Province, to PC, CRP.

26. Ibid., Page.

27. Tomlinson, safari diary, 5 February 1938, Magu and Sima Chiefdoms, CRP. He was commenting on a *New Statesman* article on India.

crime would not go unpunished, law or no law. The murderer was expelled from the district and kept under surveillance in the place where he settled afterward.

In defending what they conceived to be the rights of their people, DOs often seemed to be propping up tradition for its own sake. Some of them consciously did so. Hignell was acutely aware of the sufferings of the Gogo people during the war, and this, together with his own personal inclination to leave things as they were and not interfere with people's lives, made him oppose any scheme in the Central Province that tended to upset established ways. One DO went so far as to advise his people not to pay tax. But essentially the supposed conservatism of officers was a function of their brokerage role, of the practical need to strike a balance between letting things slide into stagnation or chaos and taking so firm a line that it put people's backs up and made an administrator's job impossible for him. Islam was strong enough in the Lake Province that officers sensibly deferred to it in the matter of European education. When the PC stopped a school being built, the local education officer naturally opposed him on the ground that gangs of boys in Mwanza were entirely neglected and therefore became the targets of agitators from Uganda. The PC could point to many cases of local opposition to the educational work of the White Fathers, and education officers could reply that rural schools managed by DOs using public funds were not as efficient as mission schools or those run by the Department of Education itself in urban areas.[28] Similarly in Masailand the DO had German Catholics on one side of him and tribal elders on the other. In 1930 permission was given for the missionaries to start a small experimental school at Longido, but the elders gave it "no support at all," and the DO had to keep the disappointed Europeans from pushing too hard.[29] The most publicized educational moves of the government itself moreover could not help looking conservative. The school for the sons of chiefs at Tabora would naturally remind everyone of the work of Vischer and Gowers in Northern Nigeria and was sure to

28. Superintendent of education, Mwanza, to director of education, Dar es Salaam, 5 April 1929, A. Cf. DO Mwanza to provincial education officer, 25 March 1949, A.
29. Monduli District Book, Murrells, 26 June 1931, and Baxter, 23 August 1933.

draw the fire of those who saw Christianity or democracy as absolute goods that would be an undoubted improvement on everything African. Yet the administrative officer had to live all day with Africa as it was and try to better it on its own lines. Idealism and alien abstractions, unless closely controlled by the government and accepted by the local people, could be disruptive and self-defeating.[30] Overall, relations between the government and educators were good.[31] But the tension between their respective tasks—keeping order versus bringing change—was undeniable.[32]

With others such as white settlers and non-African commercial people there were constant exchanges that further accented the DO's protective function. The day would come when Asian traders would be looked back on with something akin to friendship, but in the prenational time most of them were seen as sharpers who charged too much and in general took advantage of the unsophisticated African. "Kenya merchants, holding . . . a monopoly of the Loliondo trade, keep prices higher than they should be," complained a DO in Masailand.[33] The traders were a poor type of Sikh who preferred a small turnover and quick returns. The African buyer paid more; the Asian did not do as well as he might have done with a more enlightened business outlook; and the economy of the area barely ticked over. In Kahama the DO knew that Indian traders dealt in barter only and had the African at a serious disadvantage. Farmers had no real alternative to selling their produce to the Indians, who could set their own prices on goods that might or might not be attractive at the time when transactions had to be made.

> I . . . issued an order that groundnuts would only be sold in markets for cash, and a date was given for the Kahama market to open. . . . On the appointed day several hundred . . . Nyamwezi

30. Whybrow diaries, CRP. Cf. administrative officers, Lake Province, May 1927 ff. regarding accusations of Protestant groups that the government was against their educational efforts and churches, including the work of a native padre; and Page-Jones, ibid., 18 May 1956, writing as the member for local government in a circular to all missionaries, noting that such activity as food buying must be "subject to the approval of the District Commissioner," A.

31. See the Bagamoyo District Book on the Mandera Mission; and the Rooke Johnston MS on the White Fathers in the Western Province, e.g., at the memorial service for King George V.

32. See the Moshi Annual Report, 1936, accusing local missionaries of aiding demogogues against the Kilimanjaro Native Cooperative Union.

33. Priddle, 9 August 1933, Monduli District Book.

arrived with their headloads of groundnuts. The Indians refused
to buy. I told the Africans to have nothing to do with barter
and . . . I informed the merchants that unless they bought for
cash I would issue a trading licence to the Native Authority. This
was too much for them. Buying began and during the next few
weeks there was a flourishing trade.[34]

Toward the settlers there can be little doubt that most DOs had
at best an ambivalent attitude. They were, it is true, fellow Europeans. Moreover they were in a small minority by comparison with
the position in Kenya or Rhodesia, where administrative officers
who defended African rights often felt like poor relations or even
traitors to the breed. But, again, the whole purpose of the DO and
his reason for being in Africa contrasted with that of the settler, be
he British, German, Greek, or some other. In a place like Arusha
the very presence of settlers, though many DOs got on well enough
with them, cast a shadow over relations between the administration
and the people, a situation that would have been unthinkable in
most other parts of the country.[35] There was increasing pressure on
land in the Northern Province, in the Lake and in the Southern
Highlands, and of course alienation could only worsen this.[36] In the
thirties when there were rumors of Tanganyika being handed back
to Germany, DOs noted a growing truculence among German
settlers in the Iringa area.[37] Perhaps R. Bone put his finger on the
central issue when he talked of preferring gold miners in Chunya
to settlers in Iringa.[38] The miners were employing native labor too,
and they were there for money. But it was just a job to them, like
any other. The settler owned land. His presence was meant to be
a permanent thing. Yet he could not merge into the community as
one could in England. No matter how responsibly he behaved to-

34. Rooke Johnston, MS, 1932, p. 5.
35. For an example of good relations between the administration and the
settlers see Webster, acting PC Arusha, to DOs, 22 May 1929 ff., A. An illus-
tration of difficulty between the settlers and the government is given in correspondence between the chief secretary and the European Association at
Arusha; see letter from chief secretary, 15 July 1929, A.
36. Cf. Page papers, CRP, Kwimba Annual Report, 1929, in which the
DO rejected applications for land purchase from Greeks and Indians because of the pressure on land in the district.
37. Interview, Oldaker, 20 April 1965.
38. Interview, 9 December 1964.

ward his African workers, it was not likely in the long run that the two could regard the development of the country in the same way. No DO could miss seeing this. By instinct and by profession administrators stood with the Africans.[39]

The views of African life and of tribal organization that DOs held naturally grew out of the richly varied experience they had in the course of their provincial careers. During the first decade, when officers were heavily occupied with practical ethnography, many of them gained a detailed knowledge of native life that compared favorably—or so they thought—with what professional scholars could learn. "An anthropologist can know no more than a District Officer can find out and indeed he has to come to the D.O. for much of his information. There is nothing [in a recent study of a tribe in Southwest Tanganyika] that the District Officers of the 1920s did not know if they did their job."[40] Later on, the intimacy of the first years would be lessened as the presence of wives, the use of motor cars on safari, and the burgeoning of paper work cut into the time officers could devote to direct contact with rural people.[41] But throughout the whole colonial era closeness of knowledge and shades of opinion remained highly personal and not subject to easy classification by time periods or areas.[42] Everyone tended to pass specific judgments on the character of peoples in their districts, sometimes echoing the general comments of their predecessors: "The Masai is a gentleman and there is little of the time-server in him. . . . He takes some time to sum up those with whom he comes in contact. Having finally decided . . . that his trust is not misplaced, he becomes very friendly indeed, though generally maintaining a rigid reserve in regard to tribal matters."[43] Successive DOs in East

39. DOs were strictly impartial of course when hearing cases involving disputes between Africans and Europeans. It should also be noted that African and European farmers living side by side got on well, e.g., in Chaggaland's coffee areas.

40. Interview, Longland, 23 May 1965; that this was no empty boast is shown in the comparison between what DOs wrote in district books and what later was published by anthropologists who used these books; see especially the Arusha District Book.

41. Discontinuity of postings, as will be seen, was also a factor.

42. See the Bagamoyo District Book during the twenties and thirties for evidence of the controversy between DOs on specific points of native lore and custom.

43. Varian, Monduli District Book, March 1928 to July 1929, and Baxter,

Lake districts came to varying conclusions about authority within tribes and about how the British ought to proceed with reference to it. In Kwimba, Page saw power as being atomized into separate local units, each with its chief who was elected by hereditary elders.[44] A complicated interrelationship existed whereby chiefs were chosen by the elders and taught their duties by them, but whereby subsequent appointment to the hereditary position of elder was controlled by the chief. The British were wrong to try and form federations with paramount chiefs since there was no traditional basis for so wide an organization of power. Tribal cohesion in Maswa, Guise Williams thought, would be threatened alike by too direct an intervention by European officers or by making chiefs take on administrative functions they had not had before. "We have been asking the chiefs to rule directly by ignoring the heads of the village community [yet] forbidding the use of mandatory powers, fearing that they would be used in a spirit of greed or vengeance . . . to oppress the individual . . . the vital factor [of rule by consent and consultation] has been overlooked."[45] Moreover, in some areas such as Uzinza chiefs were descended from alien conquerors who had ignored indigenous social structures to the detriment of tribal morale and political effectiveness.

But in Mwanza, wrote W. E. H. Scupham, chiefs managed to take public opinion into account while at the same time exercising strong rule. Democracy was only a legend from the romantic past. It was important to remember that society was not static. His experience with the Wasukuma and the Wanyamwezi persuaded Scupham that agricultural prosperity under the British Peace was changing and strengthening political authority in the tribes in an evolutionary way and that it was up to the British to channel and influence this natural process. And Page, commenting again from Kwimba, boxed the compass of the argument by going into further detail about indigenous structures and about the effects of European rule upon them. "The real powers in the land" were the warangoma, or chiefs' representatives, who acted as intermediaries between chiefs and

---

entries of 1933, and Priddle, entries of 1932; see also Page-Jones, ibid., 1944, on Masai organization.

44. Kwimba entries, Lake Province Book; the Page entries are not dated. He was in charge of Kwimba District in the period from 1928 to 1930.

45. Ibid.

community elders. Within the stability of colonial rule, chiefly power, as wielded locally by warangoma, was rising. British demands on the whole complex of African government, from chiefs through intermediaries to headmen and elders, were irreversibly changing its nature and functions from what they had been in precolonial times. Organized campaigns of bush clearance, antierosion measures, and inoculation of cattle called for new impulses and responses, and the playing out of these responses was watched and supervised by British officers. A much more systematic organization of courts and tax collection further accented the hierarchy and gave more authority to central bodies than the old system had. To Page the effect was not totally to overlook or prejudice village mechanisms of government. Rather it put to good use the only instrumentalities—chiefs, Swahili clerks, representatives, and headmen—that were available for European-style projects. One hoped that in time local bodies would also modernize to an extent and would be able to play their own roles in schemes that were beneficial to whole districts. Tradition had great force at all levels. Chiefs and their followers were changing more than were village elders because the British were thin on the ground. By staying out on safari for the better part of every month the DO could regularly visit all the important chiefs in his district. He could never hope to see more than a small percentage of the hundreds or thousands of tribal elders.[46]

In places where chieftancy was weak the differing viewpoints of DOs were yet more crucial in determining the standards of performance that chiefs and lesser authorities were expected to meet. J. Cheyne in Dodoma brought about the removal of chief Ilotowa of Bahi in the Gogo area for general incompetence and for extorting cattle from his people.[47] When his action was overruled by the High Court the DO stuck to his guns and ultimately had his way. Arbitrary and irresponsible behavior by a strong chief among tribes accustomed to authoritarian rule was a difficult problem that called for patient education by administrative officers. But Gogo chiefs traditionally deferred to elders, and removal of a chief was managed through them rather than through officials farther up in the tribal hierarchy. Cheyne built his case against the offending chief

46. See the Arusha District Book, entries of the twenties and thirties, e.g., on tribal government, land alienation, stocking of streams, and native courts.
47. Correspondence, 13 June 1933 ff., A.

by holding barazas in which he could consult the people themselves
and by meeting with elders. Yet a later DO, Leakey, who was of
like mind to Cheyne on the need for strong British discipline, was
defeated by the PC when he tried to punish a subordinate African
official for a more minor offense.[48] The PC, Hignell, was also reluctant when the same DO wished to remove a chief.[49] The question
again was how much to interfere with tradition by insisting on
standards alien to the locale. And related to this was the question
of the probable effects of such interference. Once more, we see
the tension between custom and reform. Many DOs who were
instinctively on the side of modernization nonetheless held back
in the thought that hasty or severe action might do more harm
than good.[50] It was a matter of gauging each unit's capacity for
change and of avoiding methods that would be self-defeating. There
were always officers who preferred not to push at all. To them the
job was protection, not guidance toward something new.

In much of the work that DOs initated or pursued on their own,
the views they entertained of native rights and of what kind of
society should be aimed at tended to remain implicit, unvoiced or
unexplained, even to oneself. Often things were done from reasons
that sprang from an officer's personal interests combined with opportunities peculiar to the district where he found himself. The work
day was full of jobs that apparently had little to do with anybody's
overall plans or with deep reflections on the African future. There
was the Golden Rule, true enough: "Thou shalt collect thy tax;
thou shalt not worry thy government." Everyone got the same circulars from Dar es Salaam and filled up the same kinds of returns,
and all cadets went through the five-finger exercises of language and
finance and of three kinds of law. But with the routine satisfied,
one's attention was inevitably drawn to the limitless potential for
agricultural and other development that every part of the country
provided. In the Central Province it was a long line of DOs who
started creameries and did the necessary organizational work on the
clarified butter industry after its founding by a veterinary officer.
The idea of planting cotton in parts of the province was rejected
because officers felt that the world market, already saturated, would

48. Ibid., 4 October 1934.
49. Ibid., 19 October 1934.
50. Ibid., 2 February 1937 and 13 May 1938, Longland and Lake.

not support this and because the people of the area were pastoral and could not be depended upon to look after a cotton crop. Instead, on Hignell's initiative, attention was given to trading settlements and a type of market economy that was suited to tribal life. A. H. Pike worked out a tobacco cooperative in Songea, G. W. Y. Hucks concentrated on the production of gee in Musoma, and A. T. Culwick on rice in mountainous parts of the Northern Province. The Sukuma Land Development Scheme was R. S. W. Malcolm's brainchild and the name of C. C. F. Dundas will always be associated with the Kilimanjaro Native Coffee Union. Numerous farming enterprises on a smaller scale were constantly being set in motion by DOs lucky enough to be in relatively quiet surroundings. When he was at Korogwe, B. W. Savory was occupied with a steady stream of white men whose businesses required the bureaucratic attention of the DO. But in sleepier Pangani he could indulge his favorite pastime of starting cassava plantations, confident that no one would notice except a friend in the Agricultural Department at Tanga who gladly helped him out. When the Masai asked during the 1939 war how they could support the Allied cause, it was H. A. Fosbrooke who worked out a cattle-buying and meat-packing scheme that ultimately benefited both the government and the Masai as well as contributing to the canning industry in Nairobi.

Though no two officers were alike, it is possible to discern a basic division of the provincial administration into two general types: those whose work made for material progress and those who for one reason or another did not add much to this process. A number of officers were judged by their peers to be mere passengers. Some were conscientious enough but lacked the energy or imagination to do more than satisfy headquarters on routine matters. The majority worked hard and made a dent of some sort in the formidable and at times seemingly impervious mass that was Africa.

One DO in a southern district during the early thirties distinguished himself in the wrong way. Determined to get promotion by giving headquarters an impression of boundless industry in such areas as bush clearance and public works, he ran roughshod over natives who stood in his way and treated his European subordinates badly as well. When a cash box containing a thousand shillings of tax money was lost, the messengers responsible for it were taken into police custody under suspicion of having stolen the money.

His police asked and received the DO's permission to question the prisoners by traditional Angoni methods, which the officer knew to involve systematic torture. The men were trussed up with bamboo and thongs attached to heads and fingers and then beaten in such a way as to break all their fingers and severely lacerate their heads. Confessions were duly obtained, but an Asian recruiter of labor who hated the DO managed to leak the story to a newspaper in Dar es Salaam. The officer was promptly relieved of duty and afterward discharged from the service.[51] The whole administration stood aghast at so flagrant an exception to the rule of humane and responsible government.

Far more typical were developers of the Rooke Johnston type, who, if they were not invariably gentle, always kept the best interests of their people well to the fore. The basic division was not between the rough and the benign but between those who pushed for European-style improvements and those who did not. Some had a philosophy to underlie daily action. J. F. R. Hill saw economic progress as the key to everything, an engine that would bring social improvement quite organically, regardless of official policy, while Longland had less democratic, more Churchillian thoughts of "making the Territory fit for heroes to live in." This would place the accent on a capable leadership as the best and vital ingredient in so backward a place. But most DOs did little musing on such distant perspectives. They kept busy with immediate tasks, doing what they could in the service of finite, tangible aims and using whatever instruments could be got hold of locally. Government slogged along constructively, unspectacularly, and steadily in its homely grooves.

51. This case, which is well known to ex-Tanganyika officers, was described to me by the officer whose difficult duty it was to replace the discharged DO. It is not necessary to name either of the officers involved.

CHAPTER FOUR

Headquarters and Native Administration

The relationship between policy and practice is always a difficult one for the student of past events to get a grip on. Records left behind, in the first place, often serve to blur dead facts by being partial or overly explicit. A governor's speeches to his Legislative Council will be highly precise as to what he wants his subordinates to do. Ordinances and policy guidelines will make clear what the rationale of the exercise is to be, and the written responses of underlings will naturally address themselves to the official line, will appear to conform to it and follow it loyally and efficiently. In fact, however, there may be great distance between the word and the deed or large variation from place to place and in time periods, all of this making for a highly complex picture in which policy is to one man nothing like what it is to another. At best the official papers of colonial government—reports, returns, circulars, and office correspondence —give to policy far more importance than it had in actual practice.

Second, there is the outlook of those—mainly professional academics—whose business it is to write history. We have come a long way from the Middle Ages when some chroniclers knew little more than the inside of the monastery. But many of us retain monkish characteristics still. And the cloister today may be an even less ideal vantage point from which to try to comprehend how men felt and what they did in the hurly-burly of bush administration decades ago in another part of the world. The most obvious danger is that bookish historians will take the surviving papers at face value and will see colonial administration as some teachers of political theory see their subject: as a series of pronouncements and jottings that accurately reflect what went on, rather than as pieces, not perhaps the most important ones, in a bigger puzzle. There are two main reasons why some students of the Reformation still lecture as though Martin Luther's sermons were the whole story: first because the sermons have in fact survived, whereas much else has not; and second because the lecturer's own views and experiences of life are such as to emphasize theory.

An appreciation of the role and importance of official policy in Tanganyika depends first on awareness of the DO's relations with his immediate superior, the PC. A diagram can be drawn easily enough with little boxes connected by lines showing how everybody stood in the hierarchy, the PC at the top and all DOs subordinate to him.[1] Officers in charge of districts were magistrates, and they dealt with the High Court directly, not through the PC at provincial headquarters. As subaccountants they corresponded directly with the Treasury. If he had a police detachment in his district, without a European officer being present, the DO was himself in charge and kept in touch with police headquarters in Dar es Salaam on such matters as supply and discipline. As regards technical and professional officers the position was complicated, but in general the departments of agriculture, forestry, public works, etc., in Dar es Salaam tended to bypass PCs and deal directly with DOs, both sides hoping that individual DOs and technical officers in the districts would get along well enough to obviate rigid definitions of ranking and responsibility in each instance.[2] When the Secretariat did generalize on this subject it was at pains to make clear that "instructions are issued to facilitate, and not to hamper, the conduct of public business, and they must therefore be interpreted broadly . . . the principle being to relieve the PC of unnecessary routine . . . without impairing authority."[3]

Though they were senior to DOs in age, experience, rank, and salary, PCs were essentially coordinators, reviewers, and bureau-

1. I thank Mr. F. Longland for drawing a chart of this kind and sending it to me with his letter of 4 October 1965.

2. Eventually technical departments established their own offices at provincial headquarters, and DOs dealt with these on matters affecting their districts.

3. Acting PC Arusha to DOs, quoting Scott in Secretariat Circular no. 70, 1926. "The object [is] to leave the Executive Authority in the hands of the District Officers." Chief Secretary, Scott, to administrative officers, 21 December 1925, A.

cratic heads who depended on DOs to run their districts, while keeping PCs informed and occasionally referring important matters to them for advice or instruction.

Within this general context personality and interpersonal relations determined how much the power of the DO was inhibited by his PC.[4] Some PCs had firm ideas about native administration policy. P. E. Mitchell when PC Northern Province wrote long dissertations to his DOs on how to handle native custom, although in practice he usually agreed to their proposals and did not overrule their day-to-day management.[5] But J. L. Berne in Iringa rode P. M. Huggins, DO Tukuyu, hard on the structure of native courts: "It appears that you have gone beyond the scope of my original instructions . . . instead of working out details of a common council you have devised what appears to be a sort of soviet, which is quite inappropriate."[6] The DO fought back, even quoting the chief secretary in support of his case, but the PC prevailed. In countless small instances stronger-minded senior officers made their wishes known and commanded at least an outward deference. Bagshawe was never a man to be trifled with. But overall, DOs held sway in their districts and PCs either accepted this as the normal thing or, in asserting their undoubted legal superiority, contented themselves with observance of written proprieties by DOs. Cheyne as PC Southern Highlands was more outspoken with I. L. Robinson, DO Iringa, than his predecessor had been, yet Robinson's running of the native authority (NA) did not change materially on that account.[7] The provincial correspondence is full of instances wherein PCs openly admitted DOs' local discretion and knowledge: "It is difficult for me to advise you on this . . . you will have to rely on the feeling of the local people."[8] And again: "I will fall in with any arrangements you may make."[9] Some DOs were out of touch with their PCs for as much as five months of the year.

As PCs were bureaucratic coordinators in their provincial head-

4. Note the differences in PCs' approaches in, for example, handing-over notes, Dodoma, 12 December 1939 ff., A.

5. Hallier, DO Moshi, and Mitchell, acting PC, 14 April 1927 ff., A.

6. 7 February 1934, A.

7. 23 December 1940 ff., A.

8. PC Mbeya to DO Iringa, 13 December 1939, A.

9. I.e., on planning what the PC will see when he comes to the district on safari. PC Central to DO Kondoa, 20 April 1942, A.

quarters, so the Secretariat in Dar es Salaam was a coordinator for the whole territory. The differences in outlook and activity between DOs and their office-bound colleagues in the capital were considerable, and an understanding of the effectiveness of colonial policy is heavily dependent on appreciating these. Officers in Dar es Salaam who managed day-to-day correspondence with provincial administrators were usually junior to DOs in rank and length of service, and both sides were conscious of the prevailing authority of the DO in his district. Occupied as he was with concrete reality, the DO quite naturally saw Secretariat people as distant bureaucrats, almost as innocent of bush administration as were Colonial Office officials in London. Many of them were thought to know little of what went on "west of Kassim's."[10] The main difference between Secretariat service in a colony and service in London, according to a DO quip, was that Secretariat wallas sat under an electric fan and had their tea brought to them by black men, whereas in London one sat before an electric fire and had tea brought by white men. As he slogged along doing whatever came to hand, it was only natural that the DO would smile, or groan, according to his mood, at headquarters' latest legalism—"when the Administrative Officer wishes to act . . . he will have to see whether the power he wishes to use is limited by the [appropriate] ordinance."[11] It seemed that Dar es Salaam always saw things in policy terms, putting paper above people, and indeed the Secretariat sometimes said so quite openly. Mitchell in the twenties blasted the tendency of provincial officers to run their districts "not by administrative measures but by the personalities of the officers in charge."[12]

When governors went on safari this impression of Dar es Salaam as a never-never land of unreality could be strengthened by Their Excellencies' limited grasp of local conditions. A governor touring Tabora in the early thirties insisted on chairing a conference of local administrators and missionaries called together to discuss the current campaign against sleeping sickness.[13] Not having read the

10. Kassim's was an Indian shop on the outskirts of Dar es Salaam.
11. Attorney general to PC Arusha, 20 March 1926, A.
12. 16 March 1927 to Arusha. "I have always endeavored," he continued, "to withdraw the Administration from the 'personna' atmosphere to . . . Administration by custom, procedure and authority alone," A.
13. Rooke Johnston, MS, p. 7; cf. Whybrow diaries, vol. 1, 1926 to 1928, CRP.

pertinent files beforehand, however, he could contribute nothing, and the conference wallowed pointlessly until the governor tired of the proceedings and took his leave.

It was not always a case of "them and us" however. Many officers served in both the provincial administration and the Secretariat at various times. They helped bridge the gap in particular instances, relying on good humor and a common-sense realization on both sides that cooperation was in everybody's best interests. Mitchell, when secretary for native affairs in 1931, was not particularly impressed to find that Rooke Johnston, DO Nzasa, could produce no files when showing Mitchell and his party through the boma. The DO never bothered to file anything, preferring instead to answer important letters by writing on the back, returning the original, and throwing everything else away. But knowing that the DO had a firm grip on essentials, Mitchell laughed off his rather unorthodox office procedure. When he asked Rooke Johnston whether he would like to serve in the Secretariat during his next tour and the DO replied, "hell no," Mitchell took no offense.[14] Long-standing personal friendships also bridged the gap, there being many opportunities for officers to do each other favors. Secretariat officials responsible for postings could and did help DOs with assignments to districts they wanted for special reasons such as nearness to a doctor when a baby was expected or a natural wish to avoid a second tour in some disagreeable place. DOs for their part could give priority to particular requests for information when they came from Secretariat officials who were personal friends.[15]

The nub of the matter was that DOs and Secretariat people, though they often got on well and cooperated in official activity, lived in different worlds. With poor communications and virtually no money available that Dar es Salaam could allocate for projects imposed on DOs, the essential role of the Secretariat remained that of an overseer and receiver of reports on routine matters. They could suggest, advise, and propound official lines. Legally there could be no question that DOs were obliged to follow instructions from Dar es Salaam. But there was always disparity between the

14. Interview, Rooke Johnston, 20 January 1965.
15. Conversely, Dar es Salaam could take a practical view, as when "the DO's nightmare," the League of Nations Return, was done away with. Savory notes, 17 March 1965, p. 17.

legal and the practical positions.[16] As DOs were in fact in control, the conflict between reality and constitutionalism often resulted in situations of make-believe. "Somewhat cooked returns" were sent in by DOs anxious to keep up appearances, to make it seem that the things they did were in line with official policy.[17] The officer who used part of his medical vote for road work was only indulging in the kind of "goat bagging" that everyone had recourse to sooner or later. Artful adaptation allowed people to do what was necessary and sensible in the districts without upsetting Dar es Salaam.

This situation of DO government loosely coordinated by a light-handed Secretariat was seen as unexceptionable by the average governor of Tanganyika, and for the most natural of reasons: it was the British colonial way, roughly the same style and system as other African territories lived with and similar to those of places farther afield in Southeast Asia, the Pacific, and the Caribbean. The outstanding exception was Sir Donald Cameron, who served as governor from 1925 to 1931. While he too functioned according to the established pattern in many ways, Cameron gave more than the usual amount of thought to techniques in relation to aims, to measures decided on in Dar es Salaam and put to work throughout the territory in the service of an overall rationale.[18] It is therefore by looking at Cameron's policy of native administration, as the DO saw it, received it, and either did or did not follow it, that we may best measure the importance of high-level intent as an influence on day-to-day rule. Gauging the factor of policy may also provide a closer view of the DO's relations with Africans, especially native leaders and government employees in his district.

The governor's aims are quite clear despite the fact that most of his papers have not survived. A few letters are available, as are his published apologia and the official papers of the Tanzania Na-

16. See for example Cameron, quoted by Mitchell, 20 October 1925, to senior commissioner, Arusha, on DO powers; also minute by governor, 9 October 1934, to Lindi on the fact that everything depended on DO implementation or initiative, A.

17. Tomlinson diaries, 7 December 1937, Bukoba and Sukumaland, CRP.

18. For insights into Cameron's own views I depend largely on his correspondence, e.g., letters to Lugard, 11 October 1929, 14 August 1930, and 11 November 1930, privately held. In the 11 November 1930 letter Cameron says that the administrative officers are "wholly in favor" of his policy and that the chiefs "value it exceedingly," so much so in fact that the system would survive if the British left Tanganyika immediately.

tional Archives. Tanganyika was to be given a system of native administration not unlike those of Nigeria in whose Secretariat Cameron had served from 1908 until his departure for East Africa. In order that local society might be strengthened so as to be able to stand on its own feet in the modern world, chiefs and other indigenous leaders were to be provided with more systematic instruments of administration.[19] Each unit would have an annual budget. Revenues would be controlled, at first by DOs, and then increasingly by local treasuries as they gained competence. Courts would be modernized. Ultimately all the usual activities of local government—education, road building, bush clearance, police work, public health, and agricultural improvements—would come under the native authority (NA).

Before reaching Dar es Salaam the new governor had formulated his plans. On arrival he met with senior administrative officers and explained what was to be done. Soon the necessary ordinances and regulations for gazetting NAs were drawn up and instructions sent to DOs in the districts, everyone being eventually supplied with details in the famous "little brown books," which were Cameron's version of the classic Political Memoranda of Sir Frederick Lugard in Nigeria.

On safari the governor explained to DOs that they knew far too little of native custom, the essential base on which sound administration would have to be built, and that intensive study would be necessary before officers could put the new system to work. In areas where chiefly authority had remained fairly strong all through German times and through the Byatt years it would only be necessary to reorganize this and support and improve it. Elsewhere derelict leaders would be rescued from obscurity and rusted institutions would be refurbished. Visiting Songea, Cameron instructed the DO, Longland, to inform the long powerless and drunken chief of the Wangoni that he was "a big man now" and would be expected to

19. It is interesting to contrast this general aim, common throughout much of British Africa, with the underlying assumptions of Portugal's policy. General d'Andrade, Portuguese representative on the Permanent Mandates Commission of the League of Nations, delighted in jousting with his British colleague in this regard, questioning the wisdom of Britain's policy of making the African a better African, and holding instead that he should be made more European (see for example PMC Minutes, 6th session, 1925, p. 126, and 9th session, 1926, p. 137).

lead his people again.[20] On a large map of the territory in the governor's office districts were colored red as each new NA was gazetted, and by the end of Cameron's second year all but two were so colored.

Conditions throughout the country varied greatly, but it is possible to group the NAs into two broad categories of weaker and stronger. Within the former group were tribes that had considerable cohesion of the ethnic, economic, and geographical kind but lacked strong central leadership; others that were weak both socially and politically; and peoples whose societies had been so diluted by contact with various invaders and settlers that they hardly qualified as integrated tribes any longer.

Along the coast in the Southern Province officers knew they faced an impossible task, since local peoples had no strong leaders of their own and had become so accustomed to rule by Swahili akidas that the whole area was sunk in apathy and docility. The PC, Turnbull, had formerly served in the Lake Province and had tried unsuccessfully to persuade the governor that even in that land of conquering chiefs the new policy would face major obstacles.[21] He now invited DOs around Lindi to advise him on local peoples' capacity for more self-rule but suggested candidly that the prevailing passivity probably meant an indefinite continuation of DO rule.[22] F. H. Page-Jones, replying from Mikindani, noted that every village was under its own elders, that no central authority existed and if there had to be an NA it should be "a grouping of villages with an Akida or Jumbe primus inter pares."[23] A court structure of sorts was tacked together, but it was corrupt and inefficient from the start. Years later DOs found that traditional adjudication continued sub rosa, that peculation was rife, and that punishment was self-defeating since the guilty NA officials remained popular and were in any event irreplaceable.[24] On a small island off Kilwa it was the same. In a

20. Interview, Longland, 2 February 1965.
21. On Cameron's knowledge of bush facts, see Sir Philip Mitchell, *African Afterthoughts* (London, 1954), pp. 104–106. It should not be implied, however, that the governor was totally blind to reality. On 3 November 1925 he circularized administrative officers to the effect that NA weaknesses in some areas would necessitate a continuation of DO authority. A.
22. 7 April 1926 to DOs Lindi and Mikindani, A.
23. 7 May 1926, A.
24. DO Mikindani to PC, 15 April 1930, 20 October 1930, 17 May 1932, A.

population of only a few hundred there were more than twenty separate clans. Order had been preserved by a Swahili jumbe as far back as anyone could remember. When an NA was instituted, against the recommendation of Hill, the ADO, and on Dar es Salaam's insistence, it became a useless facade, with the old system going on underground.[25]

Among the Zaramo of Bagamoyo District above Dar es Salaam a superior NA was appointed with a paramount chief, five subchiefs, and forty jumbes, the governor observing with satisfaction that a good harvest was attributed by the subchiefs to the "return of their country to them."[26] But the structure proved a sham, utterly at variance with tradition and basically unworkable.[27] By the late thirties officers were urging that facts be faced and that an akida system be brought back as in Morogoro.[28] Even the high officials of the NA continued to defer to the old liwali in Bagamoyo, though he had ceased to hold any office.[29]

The prospects looked brighter in the Kibongoto area of Moshi District, where, carrying out the governor's instructions, F. C. Hallier, the DO, spent four days patiently explaining the requirements. The Chagga, although lacking a tradition of central chieftancy, were more enterprising than coastal peoples and did at least possess some geographical and ethnic cohesion. After the governor had approved the resulting NA, however, the DO discovered that the whole nominating process, though outwardly democratic, had been engineered by a boma clerk, acting as his interpreter.[30] After further barazas Kibongoto was united with neighboring Machame, a solution that preserved much local autonomy but left the DO, without whose efforts nothing would have been accomplished, still very much in charge, faute de mieux.[31]

25. Interview, Hill, 19 April 1965.
26. Bagamoyo District Book, Berne, DO, June 1927.
27. Bagamoyo District Reports, 1929–1931, A.
28. E.g., J. V. Lewis, acting DO, tour notes, 21 May 1938, and M. H. Dorman, ADO, 15 August 1938 and 18 February 1939, A.
29. See a long typed memorandum in the Kisarawe District Book, undated and unsigned, probably written about 1930, on the failures of indirect rule there and the reasons for them.
30. Correspondence between the PC and the DO Moshi, 21 June 1928 ff., A.
31. The starting of NAs in Masailand is discussed in correspondence between Murrells, DO, and the PC Northern, 28 February 1927 ff., A.; "In

Throughout the areas occupied by weaker tribes the aftermath of starting NAs tended to be roughly the same whatever the local peculiarities. In the Central Province PCs noted frankly that "as a result of the rapid institution of indirect administration" the "so-called" chiefs were really only clan leaders and they were neither competent nor unified.[32] It was inevitable that the akida system would continue, if under a new name, for hard-pressed DOs had to have an NCO class to help hold things together. Hamida Alimasi, akida at Manyoni since 1917, became an instructor to chiefs in 1926 and later a boma clerk.[33] When Alimasi died in 1931 the DO wrote that his services had been invaluable, especially after the Cameron reforms, and that NA efficiency depended completely on DO-akida cooperation, as pre-Cameron administration had done. By the 1940s elders were still choosing incompetent chiefs and still being over-ruled by DOs.[34] The chiefs were "supine," "the headmen lacked leadership," and NAs were doing anything but administration.[35] Twenty years after Cameron's policy was first propounded the PC Central wrote that native initiative had been virtually nil:

As a result there has been a divergence between the nominal and the real executive . . . [a system] very like the wakili . . . system in Uzaramo and the old style Akida and Jumbe system in Tanga . . . . I proposed to abandon pretence . . . authority resides in us [and the] frankest way to recognize this [is to] make the D.O. head of the Council.[36]

reality what I did was merely to establish and give authority to what had already existed before, although unrecognized . . . the council . . . of village elders." Compare this with Cameron, undated, in file no. 43, Masai District Reorganization, 30 March 1926 ff., A., claiming that the Masai now have a paramount chief, and a full NA. All the Masai really did was appoint representatives to deal with the British because the latter were too strong to be ignored. Interview, Page-Jones, 7 January 1965.

32. Partridge, acting PC, to Hartnoll, PC, handing-over notes, Dodoma, 12 December 1939, A.

33. African Civil Service File, Manyoni, 12 March 1931; see also DO Moshi, Revington, to PC, 29 May 1946, on a Somali who ran Boma la Ngombe from 1916 to the time of writing, A.

34. See ADO, O'Callahan, at Mpwapwa, to DO Dodoma, 16 January 1940 and 26 April 1940, A.

35. DO Kondoa to PC, 15 August 1943, A.

36. 14 September 1945, to Page, administrative secretary, Dar es Salaam, A. The DO Iringa, Robinson, wrote to the PC, 19 December 1939, "Before the Baraza an old man stood up . . . and stated that the time had now come for

Similarly the Ukaranga NA in the Ujiji area was so obviously
useless by 1934 that Mitchell, Cameron's chief of staff in giving
effect to the new policy and at the time chief secretary, gave the
DO authority to run the place himself, which of course he was
already doing.[37] In neighboring Kasulu DO government was the
alternative to exploitation of the primitive Ha people at the hands
of an NA that was as venal as it was inefficient.[38]

During the early Cameron years things fared little better with
NAs in tribes that were or had once been ruled by strong chiefs.
Bagshawe, PC Iringa, told his DOs that boma clerks would have to
be subordinated to chiefs, who "must be made to use the authority
given to them."[39] DOs, he said, were not spending enough time training NAs, which "were a farce at the moment."[40] The trouble was
that PCs, to please the governor, sometimes urged DOs to appoint
chiefs in a hurry and there was not enough time to find out how
particular appointments would set with the people. At Njombe,
where the Bena had once been under the conquering Hehe, the
major Hehe chief was allowed to pick a subchief to rule the Bena.[41]
Page, the DO, had his doubts, but was under pressure from the PC.
The result was to give new life to a moribund paramountcy. A similar expedient in Rungwe left a legacy of chiefly corruption and popular dissatisfaction, causing the DO to write some years later that
"the so-called paramountcies should be abolished, if in fact they
ever existed except in name."[42] At its worst the new system could

---

an 'outsider' to govern Pawaga as the rule of the local headmen had done
nothing except ruin the country . . . his words were applauded. Averse as I
am to appointing what can only be called a Wakili . . . I am convinced that
the people of this detribalized area want it." A.

37. Rooke Johnston, MS, p. 14.

38. Tawney, MS, p. 24. Cf. the 1929 and 1932 entries in the Lake Province
District Book. The North Mara NA was so hopeless that a DO was sent
there to open a new boma in 1929. Ibid., entries by Sillery.

39. 16 February 1926, A.

40. Diary, 23 February 1926, CRP.

41. See extracts from Njombe District Book, National Museum, Dar es
Salaam.

42. Huggins, 7 February 1934 to PC, A. See also Rungwe District Book,
extracts, National Museum, Dar es Salaam: "In the early stages too much
emphasis was placed on the authority of the chiefs and sub-chiefs, to the
exclusion of the great commoners, or mafumu." Cf. the experience of Guise
Williams in Geita District in trying to start an NA for the Zinza, whose
Tutsi overlords had long since decayed.

be ruinous by reviving old oppression and at the same time weak-
ening the DO's hand as protector of the people. In Kwimba before
NAs were started DOs and headmen cooperated closely. Complaints
were not overly difficult to air, and the chief, Masanja, was effectively kept in his place. Under the new arrangements, however,
Masanja had status, and the DO, in order to nurture the young and
unfamiliar institution of the NA, tried to defer to him as a means of
encouraging him while at the same time impressing the people with
the importance of his office. Unfortunately his newfound power
merely prompted the chief to more exploitation, while breeding in
the people a cynical feeling that British rule was bringing back precolonial oppression in a new guise. By the thirties DO skepticism
had become so strong in parts of the Northern Province that even
the most modest claims for NA efficiency were received with scorn.
When a junior officer wrote that the Council of Chiefs in Moshi District was managing its native treasury (NT) quite well and with
minimum supervision a senior officer replied "tripe!"[43] And A. M. B.
Hutt, who was left to run the district longer than usual because of
the staff shortages of World War II, despaired of "so-called Indirect
Rule" based on traditional authorities.[44] The only hope was for
greater participation in local government by the increasingly detribalized younger generation.

The picture was by no means all black. In Songea, where Longland was DO on Cameron's arrival, there had been NAs of a kind
for years, and chiefs had managed to survive even the aftermath of
the Maji Maji Rebellion. The Wangoni chief, "was a drunken old
rascal. But on regaining his hereditary authority he did make an
effort to pull himself together. . . . [T]he N.A. controlled . . . expenditure . . . it could and sometimes did turn down a project put forward by a D.O."[45]

Some thirty years later Longland had the responsibility of con-
ducting several parties of young Tanganyika chiefs on tours of Britain and was much impressed with their knowledge and ability, a far
cry from that of their fathers and a tribute to NA progress. Other

43. Draft copies of the 1937 Annual Report, with marginal comments by
DO, examined in the boma, 4 June 1965.
44. Ibid., 1941 Annual Report.
45. Notes, 26 May 1965.

officers had praise for NAs in the districts where they had served. To Savory the comparatively high competence of the Nzega NA was due to the cultural homogeneity of the population, almost all of them being Nyamwezi, and the fact that their institutions and cultural cohesion had not suffered as much from tribal raids in pre-colonial times as others had.[46] There was considerable response to Cameron's and, for that matter, Byatt's urging of federations in Sukumaland and elsewhere.[47] "In unity there is strength." This worked to an extent because it had something of a traditional base. The tribes had paid tribute to overlords before, so the British tax system was not all that unfamiliar. Federated courts offered a not unwelcome chance to meet with neighboring chiefs several times a year in a carnival-like atmosphere which everyone, including the accused, found enjoyable.[48]

On balance and in retrospect, however, the NAs must be reckoned an indifferent success at most. In the long-detribalized coastal areas Swahili and German rule had left Cameron little or no material to work with. It is true that, even there, large numbers of chiefs and lesser native officeholders received a certain amount of exposure to European bureaucratic procedure. But such training was achieved at a high cost in DO paper work, extra supervision, and loss of time from important development tasks. As late as 1945 Tawney found that his Ha chiefs still left "everything for the D.O. to decide."[49] In districts always cited as NA showplaces, order and progress de-

46. Notes, 17 March 1965. In an interview, 7 January 1965, Page-Jones comments however that he noticed little or no improvement in the interval between his two postings to Nzega, 1930 and 1934. But F. J. Lake, in an interview on 17 January 1965, made relatively favorable remarks about the progress of NAs in Sukumaland.

47. One very important federation, or "union," antedated the establishment of formal British administration over the whole territory. Hallier writes of "the union of the 24 different Chiefdoms which we found on the mountain when we occupied the Kilimanjaro/Meru area in March 1916. The Chiefs agreed to unify as the Chagga Council under an elected chairman." Letter, 14 January 1970.

48. It is interesting that the governor general of the Belgian Congo was much impressed by the Liwali's court when he visited it in Kigoma during the thirties; see Rooke Johnston, MS, p. 24.

49. MS, p. 36. Cf. the Tomlinson memorandum, 1937, CRP, which notes that chiefs had no real authority and therefore the DO was expected to do everything. This resulted, in his opinion, in indirect rule being both undemocratic and a waste of the DO's time.

pended on DOs and clerks, with the NA acting as a kind of "glove-monkey" in their hands.[50] Actual practice by administrative officers contrasted sharply with the deference to protocol and policy found in official reports, which gave more credit to NA initiative than was deserved. For years the fiction of three independent NTs was maintained in Njombe, whose hapless DO had to do three times the paper work without commensurate results in acceptance of responsibility by African officeholders. At last an unusually realistic PC told him to go ahead and combine the three. Then, turning to Chief Pangamahuti, he remarked offhandedly, "Instead of three bags I want just one; will that be good?" "Very good, Bwana," replied the chief, and the next annual report showed that the amalgamation had been effected "after discussion with N.A.s concerned."[51]

Giving the tribes a regulated and uniform system of local administration was "a brave attempt" to prepare them for modern organizational life without abruptly destroying their own cultural base.[52] Its main shortcoming was a failure to take enough account of tribal structures at the time and political institutions in particular. Building what was in African eyes an elaborate superstructure on rotting or in some cases totally decayed foundations was not an exercise that ever offered much promise. Gains in experience for relatively small groups of leaders were offset by losses in time that DOs could devote to helping the people directly and to restraining irresponsible chiefs. Compared to the strongest NAs in British Africa—those of Northern Nigeria—the Tanganyika ones made a poor showing. From first to last they had many of the disadvantages of Fulani NAs—apathetic and docile populations ruled by elites who were often alien and were more concerned with exploiting their people than with leading them—without the advantages of relatively strong Islamic traditions, high administrative talent, and considerable wealth. No tribal unit in Tanganyika came close to the state

50. Interview, Savory, 17 March 1965. See also the Bukoba Annual Report, by Page, 1936; in an interview, 7 April 1965, Page noted that everything depended not on the Bukoba chiefs but on the DO and on "Mwami" Lwamgira, secretary to the Chiefs' Council. The Mwanza chiefs were "lazy and given to over-indulgence in liquor." DO Mwanza, Gilbert, to PC, 4 January 1940, A.
51. Savory, referring to the events of 1938, in his notes of 17 March 1965.
52. The phrase is Longland's, notes, 23 May 1965.

organization of Kano or Sokoto. Nor did the British have as long to develop the country as they had in Nigeria.

Knowing all this full well, the average DO did the best he could to help his NA forward, meanwhile continuing to rule the district himself and struggling to avoid being submerged in paper. The 1929 depression brought staff cuts, a decrease in revenue, and a slowdown in all government activity. After Sir Donald Cameron's departure in 1931 the territory had a series of governors whose views on native administration were more orthodox and who were less inclined than Cameron had been to think they could exert a heavy influence on the day-to-day work of the provincial administration. P. E. Mitchell, who had been Cameron's chief of staff in NA matters and his liaison with administrative officers in the field, stayed on several years after the governor had left, first as secretary for native affairs, the post he assumed in 1928, then as chief secretary. The official policy of indirect administration remained in force. But Mitchell, a former DO, knew well enough what obstacles stood in the way of implementing the policy in anything like a literal way. He knew that the system could underlie but never replace DO rule. As they did in every part of Africa that was peopled by tribes with rudimentary social organization, the DOs went on running their districts according to their lights.[53]

---

53. It should be added, in fairness to Cameron, that although many officers had reservations about his policies, others did not. "We younger men held him in reverence and awe," writes one. A. Sillery, 17 October 1968.

CHAPTER FIVE

Holding the Ring

The kinds and degrees of change that came to native life over the four decades of British rule in Tanganyika differed greatly from place to place. Dar es Salaam and the other major centers altered so profoundly that political officers of the years immediately following 1914 would hardly have recognized their physical appearances, not to mention the mentality and the occupations of their people. Remote areas such as the southerly part of the Western Province or the hill country between Lindi and Mahenge on the other hand would have appeared virtually unchanged, and the tempo of life in small settlements and in open country would have seemed basically the same as in the days of the Germans.

Most tribesmen continued to cling to their own ways, resisting innovation to the last. Attempts by the DO Kondoa, T. M. Revington, to promote voluntary grain storage were unavailing, and compulsion had to be used.[1] This had the depressing effect of relieving the people of responsibility and of adding to the DO's burdens without offering the long-term advantage of inculcating habits that were in the community's interests. As the number of administrative officers available for supervising sound agricultural methods declined during the 1939 war, areas formerly cleared of tsetse gradually relapsed again to their former state, soil erosion increased, and food production suffered in consequence. NA efficiency was as low as ever, most chiefs and headmen taking little or no initiative. Too often the few vigorous, effective chiefs were also oppressive and unpopular, their natural excesses now being less subject to British discipline. When the war ended and Commonwealth Development and Welfare funds at last gave a rejuvenated administration the wherewithal to push development schemes, DO initiative was still the only way. "With the aid of special supervision, constant touring and propaganda," much could be accomplished, but "if we . . . rely

1. DO to PC, 15 August 1943, A.

on purely voluntary cooperation by . . . tribesmen . . . we are likely to have a long wait."[2]

Still, if the country people did not change one noticed differences among many who stood outside tribal life altogether and among others who appeared increasingly disaffected from it. Young men who had left the countryside for work in Mwanza and Bukoba listened with interest to what other young men said who came over the border from sophisticated Uganda. They criticized the chiefs and white men and spoke of a modern Africa that would dispense with both.[3] In Moshi, whose Chagga people were notorious for their courtesy, a gang of younger tribesmen interrupted the DO's remarks in baraza.[4] They came to the boma next morning to apologize and things quickly settled down again. But the incident was a straw in the wind and it did not go unnoticed.

It was not just hotheads from Nyasaland and Uganda who queried the status quo. For years a chasm had widened between traditional authorities and those who for one reason or another—European education, experience of missions, commerce, or government offices —felt less and less identified with them and with the past generally. Commenting on a decrease in the amount of land being farmed and a corresponding rise in food prices, the DO Bukoba wrote, in the mid thirties, "the real difficulty is not lack of land but lack of initiative or of agricultural ambition on the part of the younger generation."[5] The mere fact of learning to write, a facility seldom acquired by chiefs, led boys to reject tribal elders as incompetent. Visiting the Dar es Salaam school in 1939, Longland watched a play, written and performed by schoolboys, that ridiculed chiefs' illiteracy and

2. Acting PC Dodoma to director of agriculture, Dar es Salaam, 8 January 1948; and see acting senior agricultural officer, Dodoma to PC, 7 January 1947, A. "In plain language this [beeswax and gum schemes] implies compulsion . . . without it the schemes could not be successful."

3. PC Lake Province, memo on trends toward more representative forms of local government, 10 July 1948, copy in Arusha boma.

4. Interview, Hill, 19 April 1965, referring to events of the 1947–1948 period. Cf. Tawney, MS, p. 14, for a description of a comparable incident in 1937.

5. Page, Annual Report, 1936, CRP; see also Moshi Annual Report, 1937, by W. S. Yates: The "present Chagga youth . . . is rapidly outgrowing, economically, his mental strength"; i.e. the process of detribalization not only creates a problem of control for traditional authorities but also raises a question whether the new men are competent to manage a different order.

their general inadequacy by European standards.[6] The officer's feeling of disquiet at this spectacle arose not out of a desire to see custom preserved at any cost and without regard for needed renovation, but from an impression that the young lacked perspective; they despised their elders, overrated their own capabilities, and minimized the difficulty of building a modern society. Frequently, derogation of the old ways did not involve substitution of a new morality to take their place. Literate Africans seemed more prone to crime than the others: "It is usually the educated native who is a thief."[7]

To DOs the problem of detribalization was especially acute in relation to NAs, because of the broad responsibilities that they had throughout society. The passing decades seemed to bring little improvement. Chiefs did provide a certain social cement, a reassuring sign that familiar institutions and ways would not be lost to rural peoples who knew nothing else and would be confused by an abrupt change to alien forms. But their continuation in a context of European supervision and a developing economy was a curiously unnatural and self-defeating thing in practice. They were not allowed their old methods of collecting tribute, dispensing justice, and giving rewards in an atmosphere of authoritarianism mitigated only by clan and tribal custom; yet the new tasks they were asked to perform were uninteresting to them, or mystifying, and they and their traditional supporters did not become educated to new roles enough to evolve local administrations of a hybrid kind, as happened for example in Northern Nigeria. It was as though most chiefs had become constitutional monarchs, stripped of the right to do as they liked and left with responsibilities that they found strange or too difficult to discharge on their own.

Had the younger generation steadily moved in at the bottom and gradually replaced their fathers after taking on European education and attitudes, the unavoidable awkward stage need not have been too prolonged. But this had not happened. Most progressive youths avoided traditional offices if they could, and those who did follow in the footsteps of their elders usually found the pull of tradition too strong to resist. They soon adopted the slothful habits of older chiefs, and their rule was in the main just as ineffectual. Some suc-

6. Interview, 2 February 1965.
7. Whybrow diaries, CRP; this undated entry is in vol. 1, 1926.

cesses were recorded. Chief Mbonani in Songea had seen army service in Southeast Asia. His view of life, his administrative assumptions, and his aims were so heavily interlarded with untraditional experience that he could be counted on to help bring his NA forward.[8] A number of hereditary rulers would continue to serve in local and national posts after independence in the sixties.[9] For the most part, however, chiefs and chiefly institutions remained sluggish in the British years. DOs were everywhere conscious of a situation of lassitude and decay. "The present political organization is too weak to deal with the changing state of the country."[10] When the governor suggested that DOs follow Buganda in transforming NAs into municipal corporations capable of managing labor contracts and other aspects of development, the usual reply was "our NAs are not ready for this."[11] It was administrative officers and the clerical cadres—called variously akidas, wakilis, etc.—aided by community leaders who kept order and made progress possible. At no time were chiefs and other NA officeholders much more than a facade, sometimes useful but seldom essential to the smooth operation of local government.

While DOs and boma staff members got on with daily administration and chiefs went their harmless, ceremonial way, strong undercurrents of change were producing ever larger numbers of new men. In Tukuyu, considered by some to have been more advanced than any tribal area in Bantu Africa outside Buganda, DOs early despaired of attracting the educated young to NA service. "At present," wrote Huggins in 1934, "tribal institutions are disregarded . . . [for] the sole object of chiefs is to use . . . [their newly acquired

8. PC Southern Province to Lamb, Secretariat, 24 November 1945, A.

9. E.g., Chief Masanja, head of provincial administration, Dar es Salaam, 1965; Chief Adam Sapi Mkwawa, speaker of the National Assembly; Chief Erasto M. Mamg'enya, minister for community development and national culture. Nyerere was himself the son of a chief in the Lake Province, and his brother, J. K. Nyerere, was regional commissioner, Mwanza, in 1965.

10. DO Arusha, Troup, to PC, 4 November 1947, A.

11. Sayres, Secretariat, to the governor, 18 April 1938, A. On the split between chiefs and the young, see Elspeth Huxley's talk to the Royal African Society and Royal Empire Society, as reported in the *Tanganyika Standard*, 11 August 1947, and Sir Rex Surridge's letter of 16 September 1947 to Mrs. Huxley, and her reply of 28 September 1947, A. The DO Arusha, Troup, and the government anthropologist, Cory, noted in 1948 that the Wameru were at last ready for a more modern NA organization, but still with an akida to hold it together. See the Arusha District Book, entries of 1948.

powers] to score over one another."[12] Insufficient provision was made for using the "ideals and aims of the ever-growing class of educated and semi-educated Africans."[13] Eighteen years later Chief Adam Sapi in Iringa was still making the same point, observing disconsolately that low salaries and insufficient real authority made most NA posts unattractive.[14] Subchiefs got ten pounds a month, which was less than a boma clerk's salary. Discouraged by the difficulties of bettering themselves through the ranks of NAs, or bored with the idea, more and more young men looked elsewhere. The presence of Europeans and Asians gave them ideas and options that had scarcely existed in precolonial times when withdrawal from tribal life meant not only social failure but probably exile or death. In Chaggaland by the end of World War II the real power of economic and social decision had "passed from the hereditary authority into the autocratic and often incompetent hands" of a few self-appointed *arrivistes*, mainly Christian converts and prosperous coffee growers.[15] To these semi-Europeanized Africans with money in their pockets and a smattering of book knowledge in their heads, chiefs and ancient tribal custom seem to be nothing more than a fossilized holdover from a detested and savage past, still propped up by perverse white men for reasons of their own but irrelevant to the country's future.

For a time the detribalized were content to prosper outside the customary social framework by entering new professions, becoming veterinary clerks, drivers, primary school teachers, or employees of Christian missions, sisal estates, or railways. Soon, however, they began to develop a separate political consciousness, if only because their newfound roles did not lend themselves easily to representation or even expression through the established European and African governmental channels.[16] DOs received communications from the African Association, an organization properly registered with the government and at first seemingly concerned only with such innoc-

12. To PC, 10 April 1934, A. This was part of a memo on tribal administration in Rungwe District.
13. Ibid.
14. Hucks, DO Iringa, to PC, 21 August 1952 and 19 September 1953, A.
15. DO to PC, Arusha, 4 November 1947, A.
16. Cf. J. M. Lonsdale, "Some Origins of Nationalism in East Africa," *Journal of African History*, IX (1968), 119–146; Ralph Austen, "Notes on the Pre-History of TANU," no. 7, *Makerere*, 1962.

uous activity as helping released convicts.[17] In Bagamoyo the African Association alternated between mild lobbying on issues considered legitimate by the British and needling the boma with complaints on flimsy pretexts and demands that it must have known the DO could not accept. He replied accordingly, either dealing patiently with reasonable points or admonishing the association for wasting his time. They objected to regulations on the compulsory milling of flour, and he replied that this was for the community's own good.[18] They criticized the government for posting a male dresser at the dispensary, insisting that a nurse-in-training would do and implying that the more expensive male employee was there to serve European women in the district, a luxury that would not be available to Africans. The DO explained the economics of the matter and denied that the presence of European women was relevant.[19] But when the association asked that fish scales owned by the Township Authority be loaned to fish sellers in the market the DO agreed.[20] He was amenable to discussing adjustments in bus fares to Dar es Salaam.[21] A polite letter from the association drew the DO's attention to fast bicycles as a danger to children and to the need for controlling dogs in the marketplace, and it ended with the phrase, "God Save the Queen!"[22] The boma was sympathetic to the association's detailed criticism of an Indian doctor.

As the forties gave way to the fifties the general tone adopted by the association—whose letterhead changed to TANU in 1955—showed that criticism was founded not on a desire for action on specific points but on the basic assumption that Europeans had no right to rule Africans. Nothing the boma said or did was taken on its merits, and all was viewed with a suspicion as coming from a regime that lacked moral justification. When the DO spoke of what the district could afford he was gainsaid by men who ignored economic facts and implicitly denied that any but an African could pass on

17. DO Bagamoyo, Bampfylde, 8 April 1939, to hon. president, African Association, Bagamoyo, acknowledging its request for an interview, TANU file, Bagamoyo, 1939–1957, A.
18. Webb, DO, to African Association, 14 May 1946, A.
19. Ibid., 16 May 1946.
20. Ibid., 31 August 1948.
21. Ibid., 6 September 1948.
22. Ibid., 31 August 1952.

such matters. The theft of TANU funds by one of its own former employees left the British, who had caught the man, in the strange position of being unable to get the cooperation of the wronged institution in seeing justice done.[23] There was no longer a single, agreed standard of right and wrong in the land, or at any rate a standard that the regime could enforce whether everyone understood it or not. Things had come a long way from the time when Gogo tribesmen hid in the hills, when Nyamwezi chiefs presented German certificates to prove their legitimacy, and when coastal liwalis stood ready to serve any new master as long as he was stronger than the old one.

There was sameness and change among the British too. One noticed that a white face no longer guaranteed respect or even deference to its wearer. Most Africans were still friendly and subordinate, but the country had got so used to the Europeans, to their foibles and shortcomings as well as their achievements, that they were not objects of awe anymore. Detribalized Africans had views of government officers very different from those their fathers had had—an ill-assorted mixture of envy, of desire to imitate or surpass, of a continuing regard mingled with resentment—and these views naturally had their counterparts in British ranks. Not surprisingly many administrators increasingly differentiated between "good" and "bad" Africans, between those whose ambitions could be realized through constructive effort within the law and those who were in some state or other of protest or revolt. Handing over Arusha District to Bone in 1947 Hill spoke of two different groups of Chaggas: "There is the Chagga Association which is led by a number of literate and intelligent [men] . . . a loyal body whose object is the promotion of good Government. There is also the African Association which does not [represent] the bulk of the better Chagga and about which I will speak to you."[24] The "most important function" of DOs, such officers felt, was to make the NAs better by bringing the new intelligentsia into them.[25] The trouble was that most youths who had been to school, those from Makerere for example, were thought more clever than educated, and they showed themselves too ambi-

23. Ibid., 7 June 1957.
24. 31 July 1947, A.
25. DO Arusha, Revington, to PC, 19 April 1948, A.

tious to be satisfied with the prospect of working in the lumbering, anachronistic NAs.

These were the years of the Creech Jones policy on democratization in the colonies, a line that was not unlike Cameron's of two decades before in that it struck DOs as being easier to propound than to implement. NAs were to be made more representative of all elements in the community by forming councils to advise chiefs.[26] In commenting on problems posed by this aim, officers showed how they felt about changing society and about prospects of unity as the era of nationalism dawned. H. H. McCleery was able to report that the Pare Council was in operation, with elected but nonvoting members such as a hospital assistant, a veterinary guard, a head clerk, and an agricultural instructor.[27] This looked all right on paper, but there was the danger that a well-organized minority might swing future elections in their own favor without regard for the still-traditional majority. Bone at Moshi agreed, remarking that democracy and demagogy were hardly the same thing and that the time was not yet ripe for full-scale European-style elections.[28]

Things were better in Sukumaland and Bukoba, where akida-like entrepreneurs eased progressives onto chiefs' councils and tried to allay fears on both sides.[29] But in parts of the sleepier Southern and Eastern Provinces the somewhat nebulous Creech Jones formulas were adding to social confusion already generated by the groundnuts scheme, and haste would have to be made slowly.[30] Among the Gogo there was "no popular demand for representation . . . at the moment."[31] Perhaps districts like Kisarawe could send missions to more advanced places such as Chaggaland to observe how the new ideas worked in practice. But the tremendous variation in social development over the whole country made it necessary, as in Cameron's time, to proceed empirically, avoiding "eutopian" (*sic*) so-

26. "Despatch from the Secretary of State for the Colonies to the Governors of the African Territories," 25 February 1947. And see Creech Jones to governor, 10 November 1948, urging an end to discussion and instructing quicker action on mass education and community development, A.

27. DO Pare to PC Tanga, 27 February 1948, A.

28. To PC, 24 July 1948, A.

29. PC Lake, memo 10, July 1948, quoting Cory, government anthropologist, A.

30. PC Southern to chief secretary, 6 September 1948; PC Eastern to chief secretary, 1 July 1948, A.

31. PC Eastern to PC Northern, 20 September 1948 and 25 April 1949, A.

lutions handed down from above.[32] DOs of the late twenties would have recognized and approved of what Northern Province officers said to one another a generation later. A bureaucratic system, called for by the new policy, would require more educated clerks than were available. Africans must be "public spirited" as well as highly literate.[33] "It is a modern idea, and a bad one, that local activities should be run everywhere on similar lines . . . [as in the United Kingdom] taking the heart and initiative out of local Government. We all seem to forget these days how we benefit from *not* having a written constitution . . . the more untidy our group of systems in Tanganyika is, the healthier it will be."[34] When they warned of dangers in going too fast, however, administrators and their professional colleagues were not merely or blindly defending the status quo. Education officers, like DOs, were aware that a light-handed approach was in effect diluting tradition without building a viable alternative.[35] Despairing of the chiefs ever being able to run a local government without supervision, a certain number of DOs were always urging that the attempt to use them in political roles should be abandoned, leaving them with customary law functions only.[36] NAs were hotbeds of *fitina* (intrigue). Their corruption and inefficiency were notorious. The sensible thing, therefore, was to leave them to their fate and concentrate on evolving a more modern system and on educating the new generation that would operate it. Hall, acting PC Dodoma, thought that a choice had to be made between democracy and benevolent despotism. The former, which he favored, would mean providing a formal means of expressing public opinion.[37] But neither Hall nor F. A. Montague and Page-Jones, who wrote on the subject, recommended junking the NAs.[38] Harmonizing tradition and modernization was their objective, just as it had been Cameron's and continued to be, however vaguely, the objective of most provincial administrators. Everybody knew the

32. DO Tukuyu to PC, 1 April 1949, A.
33. DO Mbulu, Shakleton, to PC, Revington, 20 April 1949, A.
34. Handwritten safari notes, 30 March 1949, from DO Masai to PC, A.
35. Whybrow diaries, entries of 9 October 1932 and 2 April 1933, CRP.
36. E.g., J. C. Clark, ADO North Mara, to PC Lake, 28 June 1944, A.
37. R. de Z. Hall to Lamb, administrative secretary, 30 November 1945, A.
38. E. A. Montague and F. H. Page-Jones "Some Difficulties in the Democratization of Native Authorities in Tanganyika," *Journal of African Administration*, III (January 1951), 21–27.

weaknesses of the chiefs. But would egotistical, half-educated youths be an improvement, and would they be representative of all the people?

To the future rulers of independent Tanganyika these musings of provincial administrators would of course be irrelevant, for the new men would inherit full power themselves and would found a centrally organized political system, ending such local power as the NAs had possessed. They were also substantially irrelevant to actual practice in the last fifteen years of British rule, in that DOs went right on ruling after Creech Jones as they had done after Cameron. The colonial secretary's ideas on local councils did not appear workable to the DO Arusha because chiefs and other NA officials were not interested, and the PC agreed that it was better to go slowly as always, through the give-and-take of barazas.[39] When, in the early fifties, the member of the Executive Council for local government circularized provincial administrators on democratizing and modernizing NAs, by, for example, sending chiefs on visits to Dar es Salaam, he added, "the matter is not one of great urgency, nor is there any particular advantage to be gained from general synchronization."[40] To which the DO Arusha replied, "I recommend the maintenance of the status quo in so far as [this] District is concerned."[41] Everywhere DOs continued appointing, removing, and disciplining NA officials, from chiefs on down, and the modernization of each unit through the addition of educated members was fast, slow, or nonexistent according to the inclinations and talents of DOs and their office staffs.[42] The daily stint of officers in 1960, the year before independence, involved more paper work than before; but in the essentials of DO initiative and supervision it was much the same as it had always been.[43]

39. DO, Troup, to PC, Revington, 30 July 1948, and reply 17 August 1948, A.

40. Hall, circular no. 4, 20 February 1951, A.

41. 5 March 1951, A.

42. See, for example, the correspondence between the DO Iringa, Hucks, and the PC on putting progressives on the NA staff and on deposition of the chief, 21 August 1952 and 19 September 1953; also "Memorandum on the Problem of Relations between Native Authorities and the Younger African Generation," PCs' Conference, 12 May 1945, A.

43. Interviews with DOs in bomas—e.g., with A. B. Moore, Bagamoyo, 26 February 1960, and D. S. O'Callaghan, Morogoro, 29 February 1960—and

The question whether DO government was a success or not will be answered according to the tastes and experience of those to whom it is put and of course according to the atmosphere of the time. President Nyerere has had a number of complimentary things to say in public before and since independence, although, speaking in Swahili to a large audience in the early sixties, he referred disparagingly to its excessive bureaucracy and overstaffing. African provincial administrators with whom one discussed the matter in the mid-sixties mentioned the gift of office techniques and the specific training which they themselves had had from British officers, whom they named. There is dependable written testimony, such as the account of a visit to the boma at Lindi by a deputation of Makonde tribesmen and members of the Indian community, asking that a particularly popular Mikindani DO be sent to them again on his next tour.[44] The request was undoubtedly a tribute to the officer in question, while it may also have been a negative reflection on some of his predecessors and on a system that transferred DOs too frequently.

British participants have been understandably reticent and more inclined to speak of specifics than to make sweeping or final generalizations. Longland did stress colonial government's endemic thoughtlessness of the future, its preoccupation with roads and agriculture rather than with the developing minds of the natives whose lives would be so changed by such things.[45] As a result it was easy enough for literate Africans to assume that there was nothing to running a country but typewriters and tax ledgers. Hill would agree about the myopia, but his main criticism is that there was too much talk about policies—which seemed wrongheaded or irrelevant in retrospect—and too little hard work on the underpinnings of modern commercial organization which would be in-

---

with Secretariat people confirmed one's impression that there was great continuity with the past.

44. Hickson-Mahony was the DO in question. Hallier, acting PC, reported this to the governor, 18 October 1930, A. Formal expressions of appreciation, together with engraved certificates, were frequently presented to administrative officers when their tours of duty ended. Several of these, including one from the Ismaili community of Mikindani are to be found in the Vickers-Haviland Papers, CRP.

45. Interview, 2 February 1965.

dispensable once the Africans opted for Europeanism, irrespective of British policy. An overcentralized and overbureaucratic regime, especially in later years, produced "a plethora of rules and regulations" instead of "water, water and more water."[46] G. A. Tomlinson capped the argument: "It's all the system's fault, which tries to increase . . . material benefits from economic crops without paying enough attention to the mental development of the blokes who are meant to . . . benefit."[47] The administrative officers were all right as men. But there was too little money for education "to . . . save [the Africans] some of the hell that we have had to go through to arrive at even our poor effort which we call . . . civilization."[48]

A more profitable and instructive question concerns the net effects of what DOs did in their two generations of power. This is especially so to the extent that what was planned did not happen and that what happened was not foreseen until it was too late for planners to do much about it. People spoke about African self-rule, but somewhat as clergymen talk of an afterlife: euphorically and not as a discrete end toward which one marched by definite stages. To Dar es Salaam and the provinces alike it was at best a "remote possibility," something that would not come for generations or perhaps centuries.[49] Similarly with the more immediate and tangible policy of balancing tradition and progress, the classic concern of Englishmen in Africa. Change *was* the heart of the matter, but change as watched, influenced, and participated in by DOs, not the kind of change that policy-minded governors imagined themselves in control of. Most importantly this meant continuing the work of the Germans in giving the country those externals of administrative-commercial civilization that Western Europeans have instinctively worked at since the great forward push of industrialization in the

46. Notes, 21 April 1965.
47. Safari diary, 5 February 1938, CRP.
48. Ibid., 6 February 1938.
49. The quote is from the Whybrow diaries, vol. 1, 1926, CRP. He goes on to speak of independence in "50 or 100 years." Cf. Cameron to Lugard, 14 August 1930, 11 November 1930, and 8 November 1925, privately held. A. A. Oldaker, PC Iringa was doing an alienation survey in the fifties. Early in 1960 the acting governor, Sir John Fletcher-Cooke, spoke of independence being perhaps seven years away, and his remarks were confirmed by those of other knowledgeable people in Dar es Salaam, including Abdul Karim Karimjee, speaker of the assembly, and Rashidi M. Kawawa, then a prominent labor union leader and at the present writing vice president of Tanzania.

early nineteenth century. Being Europeans, the British naturally improved communications, introduced their own currency, and set up the usual administrative apparatus, including a system of justice, much of which caught on despite its coming from alien soil. Taken as a whole this meant conferring certain elements of a common culture, hooked together by a language that was thoroughly soaked in the experience, and therefore the implicit assumptions, of European bureaucracy and the money economy. It was done by demonstration and discipline, by an educational process that was all the more effective for being unselfconscious and confident. European culture was taken up by adults who needed and wanted it because, rightly or wrongly, they regarded it as superior to their own.

Among the tribes and in the countryside generally DOs tried to prop up traditional authority, to support custom as the only sensible basis of order and of progress within order. One effect was to reassure the rural masses that their familiar ideas and ways of living would go on pretty much as always. They saw that they were to be neither abandoned nor subjected to the kind of social shock that would have to accompany a more energetically innovative rule. What this involved in practice was neither a pure form of social Darwinism, the fittest surviving by brute strength and the rest sinking utterly, nor an Orwellian totalitarianism that left nothing to chance. The Chagga infiltrated areas peopled by Arusha tribesmen, which would have happened if the British had not been there. But violence was kept down.[50] Tribal leaders were picked by DOs according to alien standards of efficiency and responsibility. But those selected were at least indigenous leaders, and an endless effort went forward to convince the masses that European standards were suited to peace, justice, and prosperity.[51] Central chieftaincy was not a Masai tradition and their tribal elders did not like the tendency of the NA system to elevate a few men, to the detriment of aggregate rule by themselves. But a new kind of life for the Masai was coming perforce, and institutions suited to primitive,

50. Cf. DO Moshi to PC Arusha, 29 May 1946 and 12 August 1946, A.
51. "The reality of respect for the position of the Chief ... depended on efficient administration of tribal laws and the smooth running of courts," which in turn depended on "the personality of the Administrative Officers and upon their adherence to the principle that true administration is nothing more than the maintenance of personal touch with every native." Moshi Annual Report, 1935, Moshi Boma.

nomadic existence would no longer suffice. It was a handful of DOs who kept order in the transition period, easing the tribesmen into new ways that their traditional elders would have opposed by violence.[52] Significantly, the process of change often outran British sensibilities about protecting tradition and their constant aim of encouraging the tribes to respect what were thought to be their own institutions. When a new chief of the Kwimba was installed in 1929 Cameron presented him with a traditional carved throne, while his own NA officials gave him a Buick.[53]

The detribalized, a steadily growing minority with power more and more out of proportion to their numbers, naturally moved faster and farther from custom than did the mainly rural majority. Instigators from Uganda and elsewhere contributed to their disaffection from the old ways. Europeans did also, especially in mission and government schools, and less deliberately in commercial firms, in government offices, and in military units. But essentially the movement was a natural one, reflecting the spontaneous, unaffected preferences of many kinds of Africans for things European. The British, whether or not they were fully aware of what detribalization meant, steadily accommodated to it. As they had been too thin on the ground, in the beginning, to do without chiefs and tribal institutions, so now they lacked power to stem the tide of Europeanization, even if they had wished to. DOs understood better than anyone how and why NAs had failed to grasp the opportunities offered them since the mid-twenties. NAs were doomed not only by the challenges of detribalization but by their own inherent shortcomings. Everyone knew by the late fifties that Tanganyika's future would be in the hands the new men. Whether Britain's general policy of native administration be called a brave attempt or a misguided one, the fact is that independent Tanganyika opted for increased modernization, and not for plans and institutions that emphasized tradition. Its people inherited the framework and the spirit of a state, within which they would someday evolve a nation. Consciously or not, the DOs who held the ring were the indispensable engineers of that framework.

52. See Hans Cory's entries, on both the Masai and the Warusha, in the Arusha District Book, undated. He quotes a number of DOs, including Longland and Fosbrooke, and cites previous entries by them in the ethnographic and native administration sections of the book.
53. Page Papers, CRP, quoting his Kwimba Report, 1929.

Excerpts from Selected
Papers

The following excerpts are taken from the collections of the Colonial Records Project of Oxford University.* Selections have been made with an eye to the overall work of provincial administrators in British Tanganyika and in the thought that no one can speak more authoritatively and comprehensively on that subject than the former officers themselves. It is fortunate, for the purposes of this volume, that perhaps no other territory in the British colonial empire, as it was constituted up to the era of nationalism, is better represented in the Colonial Records Project than Tanganyika.

In making selections, I have had in mind a number of broad categories, the most important of which are the types of documents employed and their subject matter, the main time periods in Tanganyika's history, the principal geographical and tribal areas of the country, and the kinds of men—easily the trickiest category to generalize on—whose service these documents refer to.

As regards types and subjects of papers I have thought it right to include official accounts such as annual reports, some examples of official correspondence among district officers, provincial commissioners, and the Secretariat in Dar es Salaam, one or two ad hoc treatises on particular subjects in which the government was interested, and some fairly extensive excerpts from a safari diary. The last tends to be less formal than office reports and correspondence, although officers knew that their superiors would usually wish to read their diaries or have summaries of them. I know of no other source that gives as vivid, precise, and wide-ranging a picture of the countryside and its people as can be found in a good safari diary.

* I am grateful to the owners of papers, or their heirs, who gave permission through the Colonial Records Project for excerpts to be included in this volume.

Unlike the preceding essay, the documents do not cover the earliest period of all. Rather they refer to the core period, from the late 1920s to the end of World War II, from the time when the whole country had been brought under settled administration to the years just before independence began to be considered in a systematic way.

The papers make mention of most of the major geographical areas and of a representative number of tribal groups, such as coastal peoples who had been heavily influenced by Arabs and Europeans, the peoples of the south, the north, and the northwest who had received indigenous conquest and overrule, and some groups in western Tanganyika whose primitive ways had remained relatively undisturbed in precolonial times.

As to the officers themselves, I would not claim that they are representative of the whole service in ways that have to do with personality and character; only that their aggregate service extends from 1917 to 1962, that the list includes men who served in both the districts and the Secratariat and some who never left the districts, and that the group is typically varied in educational background and military service.

F. C. HALLIER

The Union of Machame and Kibongoto, Moshi District, 1928

Hallier was born in 1888, of a county family in Yorkshire. He had lived in South Africa before serving in the East African campaign, which took him to Tanganyika, then German East Africa, in 1916. He was seconded the following year as assistant political officer in the Rufiji District near Dar es Salaam. Throughout the interwar period he served in the provincial administration as a district officer and eventually provincial commissioner. He retired in 1939, returning to South Africa.

This letter was written when Hallier was in charge of Moshi District in the Northern Province. It is in the form of a report to the provincial commissioner. The letter shows a concern that the wishes of the people be adhered to as much as possible, especially in matters of tribal organization. Administrative officers devoted considerable time, particularly in the early years, to investigations in this area.

MOSHI.
Northern
5th. October 28.

The Provincial Commissioner,
Northern Province,
ARUSHA.

. . . I have just returned from Kibongoto whither I proceeded on the 2nd. instant in company with Abdieli the Chief of Machame, his father Shangali, and the more important men of his Council. I had received information that the Wa-Kibongoto were anxious, and well disposed towards receiving their new Chief—several envoys from Kibongoto having arrived during the last month in Machame bearing tidings of good will.

Chief Abdieli received a warm and satisfactory welcome and at the introduction and reception meeting there was every token of good will and friendly references to the days when Kibongoto was ruled by men set up by the Great Chief Rengwa of Machame.

Five head of cattle were slaughtered, and dancing and singing indulged in until darkness fell on a day that should be memorable in the annals of Kibongoto.

I feel sure that the Wa-Kibongoto are now even more unanimous over the Union than they were a few months ago.

His Excellency approved of Simion as Headman of Kibongoto; this was not asked for in previous correspondence and you will remember I spoke to you on the phone anent this point, and you agreed that the Wa-Kibongoto could be told to elect a Headman if they did not want Simion.

The selection of a Headman has been somewhat in the nature of a revelation, and an indication that the Wa-Kibongoto have at last awoken to the fact that their political troubles are due to the fact that they have in their midst several sons of former Chiefs of Kibongoto, to wit, Jacoba s/o Sinare, Matolo s/o Lillo, Barnabus & Ndekiro sons of Ngalami, Simion s/o Mkunde and Simon s/o Kitika.

At a Meeting of all the Subdivisional Headmen (Wachili) Elders and people numbering some twelve hundred these former "princes" were told in no mistaken language that not one of them was wanted as Chief or Headman and that all the past trouble had been due to their machinations, chiefly because none of them belonged to a house with a long record of Rulers or Chiefs and because of the jealousy that existed between them.

Finally the Meeting, at which I was merely a spectator, after having first explained the importance of selecting a Headman, decided that they would rather not select a headman and requested me and Chief Abdieli to select a non-resident of Kibongoto.

I have consulted with Chief Abdieli, Shangali and his Councillors and they advise leaving the question of selecting a Headman for Kibongoto in abeyance for several months.

Chief Abdieli proposes to visit Kibongoto every fortnight and to carry on with the subdivisional men (Wachilis) until such time as he has gained more knowledge of Kibongoto and its people. I think this is a wise suggestion and recommend it. There will be a good deal of "cleaning up" to do at Kibongoto and I think it is best for the Chief to do it himself, it will bring him into closer contact with the Elders and people and this will have beneficial results.

A headman will certainly have to be appointed later on as the Chief being Treasurer of Haye in addition to his other duties could not possibly continue to visit Kibongoto every fortnight, consequently the proposed amended Native Courts Order can remain as already recommended by you.

Now that Kibongoto has been absorbed in Machame consideration must be given to an increase of the Chief's salary. He will certainly have additional expense to bear, for instance there will be considerable extra travelling, to and from Kibongoto during the next, say six months. The distance from the Chief's Headquarters at Machame to Kibongoto is 26 miles. The Chief's visits to Kibongoto will have to be frequent for a year or two even after a Headman has been selected. I do not suppose that the traditional "fitina" of Kibongoto will die in a day.

The additional population (i.e. Kibongoto) absorbed is 4140 which makes the total number under the Chief of Machame number 29,689, that is nearly 30,000.

The Chief is very energetic and attends personally to all public works such as buildings, bridges and roads that are undertaken in his country as well as the Haye Council Meetings once a month. I think he should be encouraged in the great energy and interest he shows in the affairs of his country and Kilimanjaro generally, and not be hampered by pecuniary considerations. I consequently, would recommend that his salary be increased by at least Shgs.1000/– per annum from 1st. instant.

The former Chief of Kibongoto received a salary of Shgs.1000/– per annum but I always thought the office, though not the man, was underpaid.

F. C. Hallier
DISTRICT OFFICER

W. F. PAGE, c.m.g.

Tour Report, Njombe District, 1928
and Report on
Administration of Justice, Mwanza District, 1932

*Page was born in 1894 and was educated at Clifton. He had
farmed in Rhodesia before World War I, during which he fought
in France. He joined the Tanganyika service in 1922 and spent considerable time in both the provincial administration and the Secretariat. During World War II, he was director of manpower in Dar
es Salaam and was briefly labor commissioner. He retired in 1946.*

*The following excerpts from an unusually rich and varied col-
lection bear the stamp of an inquiring mind and a high intelligence.
The Njombe report deals with tribal history, with boundary disputes,
and with the beginnings of indirect administration in the Southern
Highlands. The report on justice is Page's response, written while
he was in Mwanza, to a government circular asking for details on
the workings of the legal system. Among the topics mentioned in the
circular were the law of evidence, the use of English, native attitudes on appeals, the views of educated—i.e., detribalized—natives,
delays in the hearing of cases, and the costs of the legal system.*

Tour Report, Njombe District, 1928

. . . By car to Mwakete, thence on foot to the Lake, where I
proceeded by canoe as far as Chanjale, porters going overland,
canoes to accommodate my loads not being available. Had they
been so, I had intended going right down to the Upangwa boundary
at the Kilendo River, but the going was very bad for porters and
time did not allow of taking them beyond Luimbira River. I returned via Matema intending to get back up via KATUNGIRA and
MADEHANI, an easier climb, but the route was reported too heavy

going for porters owing to flood water of the RUFIRI River. The route I took in alternative to Mbenba's was a very rough and steep climb and should not be done with an ordinary porter Safari.

2.   From Mwakete the Bulongwa road was followed till the turning to Headman Ndwanga's, thence by old road to Chelelo's and on to Mwakarukwa's. Thence by native path (very circuitous) to the Lake at Ikombe, the path down to Luimbira being washed out. By native path from Matema to Utengule, thence by old German road to Bulongwa. From Bulongwa the old German roads were followed to Magoye and round to Mpumbwe, where it was left to go to Loga, another being followed from Loga to KUNGAGI hill, thence by native path to Mwakete. From Mwakete by car to Njombe.

3.(a)   On the outward journey road work on the Malangali road at Makoga was inspected, where good progress had been made in the improvement of the surface and cutting of drains on the two hills there by Gangers David and Thomas. Also work on the Lupembe road near the Mtitafu River where Ganger Yussuf had done good work.

(b)   The only bad spot on the Mwakete road was a wash-out at the bottom of Kipengere hill, where I got "stuck". This had been repaired before my return and the whole section, Mdandu-Mwakete, is now quite passable. A gang is still working on the improvement of the surface and construction of drains. The long hill up from Tandala needs surface repair. A lorry got out and back about 24th inst.

4.   I am glad to be able to report what appeared to be a much more satisfactory state of things than that which I found on my last visit. Everything seemed much more "alive" and orders promptly and properly carried out. At almost every camp everything was ready for my Safari on arrival, roads—as distinct from native paths little used—were cleaned and bridges had been repaired or rebuilt where necessary. In fact, my talk with Mwemusi on my last tour seemed to have had a greater effect than I either anticipated or intended, e.g. he had ordered bandas to be built at headmen's vil-

lages which I had not mentioned, nor particularly desired. However, though only outward signs affecting an official tour rather than actual tribal affairs, it all goes to show latent qualities which can be stirred into action with advice and encouragement.

5. Chief Mwemusi and Sub-Chief Mwalukisa met me at Mwakete, the latter accompanying me to the limits of his area and the former to Sub-Chief Chelelo's, where he left me to attend to arrears of Baraza cases due to his lengthy sojourn at Njombe last month. He met me again at Isapulamu and thence accompanied me through Uwanji back round to Mwakete. Sub-Chief Chelelo accompanied me from Mboza down to the Lake, until he fell sick at Matema on the return journey. All headmen were met or visited except Headman Sihudika.

6. The question of Subordinate Courts for Sub-Chiefs Mwalukisa and Chelelo was discussed at a baraza at Mboza all Chelelo's headmen expressed themselves in favour of a Court. His village is further from Bukwama than Mwalukisa's and his people generally extend to a greater distance. He is older and has more balance than Mwalukisa, I think. Mwalukisa lives nearer to Bukwama, as do most of his people. He does not apparently want a Court and Chief Mwemusi does not seem keen on it. He is still very young in many ways. I note from your 826/6/2/10 of 3/5/28 to the Hon. Chief Secretary that a recommendation for the granting of Subordinate Court powers to both these Sub-Chiefs has gone forward, so presume they will be gazetted in due course. If in order, I suggest the actual institution of Sub-Chief Mwalukisa's Court be deferred until the need and desire for it appears more definite. Actually, Mwalukisa is senior to Chelelo in family descent according to tribal tradition, but this point does not seem to influence the parties concerned. As I did not meet all his headmen in Baraza I do not know their collective opinions on the subject.

7. I had intended getting down to the Lake at Luimbira (Alt Langenburg), but the path being reported unfit for porters I had to take the Ikombe path, being under the impression Ikombe was more or less neutral ground. On arrival I found, however, that I was definitely in Rungwe District, the boundary between Headman

MWANDORA of Ikombe and Capitao MWANYKANIRA of Nkanda, a former Jumbe under German regime, being recognised as the PANGWINO Stream at the Lake Shore and UTALIRA hill above, about midway between the two.

8. Sub-Chief Chelelo, who accompanied me to the Lake, had previously informed me that he wished to raise the question of the country of Headmen Mwandora and Kiserero (of Rungwe) being brought back again within his area of Ukinga, it having been so in pre-European days when the LUFIRI River formed his boundary. (He apparently reported a boundary dispute with Headman Mwandora to Mr. Northcote, whilst stationed at Tukuyu, vide District Book.) As I was desirous of getting as much information about the Wakisi as possible I asked various questions as to how far they extend round the north end of the Lake and the limits of their settlements. This may possibly have helped the rumour, which apparently was going around before I left the Lake area, that I had come "kutengeneza mpaka". (Chelelo may have started or helped it along as propaganda, I do not know). I did not wish to appear to be butting into the affairs of another District (I was very careful to explain both at Ikombe and Matema that I was merely passing through these places to get to parts of my own District and had nothing to do with their shauris), so I did not ask Mwandora or his people, or cause enquiries to be made, as to what their own wishes in the matter were, but I was gratuitously informed later by an Mkisi that they welcome the idea. I merely told them at the time that any alteration of the District boundary would have to be referred to you and to the District Officer, Rungwe first.

Mwandora himself stated that he is of Ukinga origin, and that he formerly owed allegiance to Mwemusi and Chelelo his grandfather having come down from Ukinga. He now passes as an Mkisi however and stated that all his people (180 male taxpayers) are Wakisi. His boundary with Headman Kiserero is the MAFI Stream, which flows from the hills nearby, and follows the line of the escarpment, into the Lake. The line of the mountains sloping down to the Lufiri plain runs N.W. from the Lake and would appear to form a natural boundary line. The present boundary causes Rungwe District to abut on to the Lake shore in front of Njombe in the hills behind, but if this line were followed right down to where the Mafi enters the Lake, it would bring Mwandora's country within Ukinga and Njombe District, but not Kisereros. I do not see the same advantage in the transfer of this latter area, because it is on the Lufiri plain and his Wakisi are in a minority (he could not say how many he had, but apparently there is no doubt they are inter-mixed with Wanyakyusa, who predominate). He also stated he came originally of Ukinga stock, though now known as a Mwanyak-yusa. Here the boundary question was voiced by the people them-selves, Kiserero himself first saying it was "shauri la Serkali" but later coming along and saying he wished to come under Ukinga. I told him I could do nothing in the matter now without reference to the District Officer, Rungwe and if he seriously entertained the idea he could go and tell the latter about it. It may be noted in this connection that Headman Mwakarukwa (Ukinga) states that many of his people have emigrated to Kiserero's country in the plains.

9. From Pangwino River to the Kilendo River, which is the boundary with the Upangwa Wakisi, there are seven main hamlets scattered along the Shore. Under the German regime each was under a separate Jumbe but these were abolished by Major Wells. Formerly they all owed allegiance to Mwemusi. They are as follows:

NKANDA.	MWANYKANIRA	50	Wakisi male taxpayers	
LUMBIRA.	MWASONI	12	"	— —
PISSANGA.	KARIMERERA	17	"	— —
CHANJALE.	MAKASIUKA	14	"	— —
MBIMBI.	MANGAGAWA	4	"	— —
PAWOJO.	MAKABARUFU	24	"	— —
NTSERE.	MASHINGUTI	26	"	— —
		147		

Makasiuka is recognised by Mwemusi and the people themselves as the head of these, though were Mwandora's area to come in, he would be. Pissanga is only about a mile from Chanjale (the map is wrong as regards position of Pissanga). So these two may really be grouped together for numbers. At present Makasiuka appears to hold, with Mwemusis approval, an unofficial baraza for the set-tlement of minor shauris (fee being sent to Mwemusi) owing to the big climb up and distance to Bukwama. This is hardly satis-factory and as soon as the position of Ukisi generally is settled should be regularised. In this connection it may be noted the German Administration appointed an Akida, MAKANAGAMU (an Mkisi nonentity who apparently curried favour), to control the Ukisi area from Mkanda to Lupingo.

10.   All these ex-"headmen" state that they formerly had many more people, but that numbers have gradually moved across the Lake to more fertile country in the Lufiri plain. Those that remain, although they grow a little mtama, are mainly dependent for subsistence on the barter of "vyungu" for food with the Wanyakyusa. This industry is carried on by the women, mainly between Ikombe and Pamojo, beyond that Southward it is much less evident. They differ from the Wakisi of Upangwa in that, although they make gardens on the lower slopes of the mountain, they do not go right back into them in search of more fertile soil as do those of Upangwa, and therefore are not so intermixed with the Wakinga above. They cultivate much less than the latter, and are consequently much more dependent on imported food. Their cultivation is mainly on the small comparatively flat, strips along the Lake Shore jutting out here and there.

11.   It is stated that their language, Kikisi, is most akin to Kinyakyusa, and that they find difficulty in understanding Kikinga or Kipangwa at first. Here however their affinity with Wanyakyusa appears to end as their customs are dissimilar. Though having something in common with Ukinga custom, their customs are stated to be more akin to those of some of the Mbeya tribes, Usafwa, Umika etc. I could find no confirmation of the theory of Capt. McAllan's Arab informant that they originally came from the Zambesi country. The wazee [old men] state they have always been Lake people so far as they know, and the only movement has been northward and north-westwards round the Lake, primarily at the time of the Angoni invasion, from the Manda area, and more recently in search of more fertile land as already stated.

12.   Reviewing the Wakisi of Njombe District as a whole from Manda to Mwandora's area, it will be seen that they comprise approximately 450 male taxpayers in Upangwa and 150 in Ukinga, being 600 in all. It would appear to be obviously an insufficient

number to consider the creation of a separate tribal unit with its own treasury. Even if Mwandora came in, they would be a bare 800 male taxpayers. I cannot say what their numbers are in Rungwe District beyond Ikombe, whether they would be sufficient to make up a possible unit of a minimum size which could pay its way. If not, the only alternative to their remaining as they are would appear to be to recognise them as a series of village communities with a common treasury, and a Court in some central position, where the people are most concentrated, e.g. Magaga or Ikombe, canoe journeys along or across the Lake being of small import to them compared to footing it up the mountains.

13.   I instructed Sub-Chief Mwalukisa to find a suitable youth for training as a Dresser for his area. The present dresser at Sub-Chief Mwaliwali's belongs to Sub-Chief Chelelo's village. I accordingly instructed Mwaliwali to find a suitable person, who when trained will be stationed at Matamba, allowing of his present dresser proceeding to his own area for duty.

14.   Sub-Chief Mwaliwali met me at Magoye and accompanied me through his area. I gave him the opportunity of deputing his "ndogo", in view of his age, but he preferred to come himself.

All Uwanji headmen were met at Matamba where a baraza was held excepting Headman Mwafuko, who turned up at the next camp. Tax collection procedure and Native Administration matters in general were discussed.

Here again, orders appeared to be well carried out.

15.   Sub-Chief Mwaliwali states that he is of Ukinga origin and names his ancestors back through 15 generations to one NAFWA, who came from ILONGWE in the Uhehe country. This seems to agree with the version that the Wakinga originally came from that area, passing on through Nyumbanitu to the Livingstone mountains. By Uwanji custom, Mwaliwali's "ndogo", Mpelangwa (not the headman of that name) will succeed the former on his death, unless the latter pre-deceases him, in which case his eldest son Silekere (also not the headman of that name) will succeed.

16. Uwanji formed part of Chief Merere's country in pre-European days, the German Administration making Mwaliwali an independent "Sultani". Mwaliwali himself is obviously no lover of Merere, who he states is of Uwanji orgin, and short of retaining his independence, prefers to try Mwemusi's rule. Though nothing was said to me officially by the headmen or elders, I gather the people generally would rather be back under Merere with the Wasangu than under Mwemusi with the Ukinga, with whom they have less in common, either in language or custom. As no mention of this matter was made to me I made no public reference to it.

17. A case of alleged "mbuda" was reported from Headman Silekera's area. I camped there and enquired into it on the spot. The complainant was a boy of about 8 years and the suspected "mwanyambuda", a near neighbour. The result of my enquiry forms the subject of a separate report. I visited the scene of the mysterious disappearance of a man and his wife in Headman Mwafuko's area, but could find no evidence to suggest "mbuda" practice, beyond that already recorded on enquiry at Njombe.

18. I was much impressed by the apparent high fertility of parts of Ukinga, particularly Sub-Chief Chelelo's area. Here one sees plots of wheat side by side, presenting more the appearance of the intensive cultivation of France and Belgium than that usual to Africa. The men assist in the cultivation, as they do in Uwanji, and men and women together must put in a lot of work. Judging by the depth of soil evident at various places where the hillside has been cut or washed away, a good depth would appear to be general in many parts of this area. In view of the close native settlement already existing, I doubt if ordinary non-native settlement will be found to be feasible in these fertile areas, but I noted hill slopes with light forest and a fine depth of black or dark chocolate soil, which suggested tea possibilities, bearing in mind Capt. Bell's remarks at Lupembe. Large areas would not presumably be required for individual holdings for this purpose and small alienations might be found to be possible. The Elton plateau in Uwanji, judging by grasses and the height of mtama (usually not more than 4' to 5') seen, would appear less fertile, being mainly red soil. It is in parts

but sparsely populated and there would be plenty of room for non-native settlement for mixed farming. Cattle seen looked in good condition and those examined were free of tick. Eastern Uwanji appears to support but poor cultivation of any sort, being more mountainous, stony, poor bush and grasses.

19.   I mentioned the prospective wheat mill at Hagafiro at my Baraza at Sub-Chief Chelelo's, in whose area most of the wheat is grown. The distance makes them rather sceptical. If the mill owner had a buying agent at Mwakete and arranged his transport from there, I think there is little doubt that there would be increased production and that he would find plenty of sellers. At present the greater proportion of wheat grown is consumed by the growers and their immediate neighbours in Ukinga. Some Wabena come and buy, and a certain amount is carried to Malangali for sale, where the price is stated to be Shs 4/50 a bag. But the distance does not encourage this market. At Tukuyu, where the price is 4/–, there is said to be little demand now.

20.   I visited the Berliner Mission at Matema, where Mr. Konig is in charge, having arrived there in January last. He is mainly engaged on making the buildings habitable again. They are in bad repair. Pupils of the schools in the Metama, Bulongwa and Magoye areas of the Berliner Mission were seen at various villages. The average percentage of scholars able to read and write at all appears to be very low, not more than about 8%. The old question of immunity of Mission natives from tribal law was raised at Magoye. I am communicating with Rev. Priebusch on this matter.

21.(a)   Mr. Durheim of Iringa was at Mwakete for about 3 weeks buying hides from natives. He appears to have done quite good business. He is a potential applicant for a duka site at Mwakete.

(b)   I was informed that women bearing twins are exempted from liability for tax in Rungwe District, and asked if the same principle could be applied in this District. If the information is correct I personally would be quite prepared to offer the same "bounty" in this District.

(c)   There are 8 German graves at Luimbira. Formerly, a native, Kabenge, who at one time was caretaker of the old Boma buildings there, received a small gratuity of Sh. 8/– per annum at the end of the financial year, when headmen were paid their tax percentage money. Since the institution of Native Administration he has received nothing and the graves accordingly have not been attended to. I instructed him to clean them up. He might be paid a small annual fee from Upkeep of Station or similar vote.

(d)   I was apparently the first officer to visit the Ukisi hamlets between Ikombe and Kilondo River. Ikombe was last visited by Mr. Richards (1923?). The Uwanji headmen and some of those in Ukinga had not been visited since Mr. Northcote was stationed at Tukuyu. Headman Mwakalila stated no one had visited his village since Major Wells. It meant 2 extra days to get out to him and back again, no path through to Magoye being passable for a porter safari, and I had not the time, otherwise I should have visited him.

W. F. Page
DISTRICT OFFICER
Njombe.

Report on Administration of Justice,
from Mwanza District, 1932

. . . Though I presume that I am asked to report in accordance with paragraph 4 of the Circular I consider that such a report must of necessity embrace comments on some of the points mentioned in paragraph 2.

2.   The ordinary native, I believe, appreciates that the High and Subordinate Courts administer justice more fairly than he has previously been accustomed to under other regimes. If it were not for his lack of understanding of the law of evidence and procedure on which judgments are based, his appreciation would be much greater. The judgments of the Native Courts now held in public are also regarded as more just than those formerly given by a Chief

from the seclusion of his house by the mouth of an elder, or when the elders virtually decided a case themselves and frequently (by tribal custom) received a fee in kind for their labours; in both cases "the longest purse" being a considerable factor. Further, the right of appeal to the District Officer and beyond enhances the sense of justice obtainable.

3. The law of evidence and procedure undoubtedly provokes astonishment in the native mind as to the findings in many cases before the High and Subordinate Courts, particularly the former. It is a first principle of English law that an accused person is presumed innocent until he is proved guilty. In many Continental legal systems the reverse obtains; i.e. the onus is on the accused to prove his innocence and not on the prosecution to prove his guilt. Native law is in many respects much more akin to the latter system. The native cannot understand what to him appear to be laws made to the advantage of the accused and the consequent disadvantage for the complainant.

4. In native law there is no fine distinction between relevant and irrelevant evidence. Each party and his witnesses tell their story as they recollect all that happened. Irrelevant or hearsay evidence may constitute a not inconsiderable part of it. Such evidence is heard and considered in Native Courts in accordance with native law. It is accepted that when a thing is generally known and spoken about there must be something in it. When a native is giving evidence before the High Court or a Subordinate Court he frequently finds himself checked in the telling of his story because he mentions facts which are not strictly relevant. This is particularly the case in the High Court and Subordinate Courts when counsel appear, ever ready to pounce on inadmissible evidence. This upsets the witness who does not understand, with the result that he omits subsequent relevant evidence, which may thus be lost, or fabricates evidence on the lines which he thinks is wanted. The truth is required and the law as to relevant evidence should permit the Court to obtain it in the manner best suited to native psychology. A patient magistrate with some knowledge of natives endeavours to effect this as far as possible, but more latitude is required.

5.   Whilst the reasons for the very strict law as to the admission of confessions may be understood by Europeans they are not by natives. A native may, soon after the commission of a serious crime quite voluntarily confess to it to a Native Authority or one of its headmen or messengers—which latter perform the immediate functions of police in the Native Administration area. A decided case (Rex versus Masota Msembe) has held a confession made to such an Authority or its officers to be inadmissible. I was stationed in Tabora District at the time and I believe I am right in saying that in native opinion there was no doubt as to the accused's guilt. Again, a native having confessed to an offence to his Native Authority or its subordinates, he later, probably after his admission to gaol on remand, may retract it and deny to the bitter end and be acquitted.

6.   The law as to the evidence of accomplices, the reasons for which may again be understood by a European, is also difficult of comprehension to a native. It is well exemplified in cases where they may be two or more accused and little, if any, evidence for the prosecution beyond that of the complainant, e.g. stock theft cases in Musoma District. The complainant may be the only witness giving relevant evidence of value against the statements of the accused and their friends, whom they call by pre-arrangement as witnesses in defence. The weight of evidence is in their favour and they are acquitted, though native opinion, based on information which may not be forthcoming for the prosecution considers them guilty. One of the accused or defence witnesses may be prepared to "split on" the others but, as an accomplice, his evidence, though not legally inadequate, must generally, in accordance with practice in decided cases, be accepted with reserve—corroboration demanded.

7.   The attitude of natives towards appeals varies considerably. Generally, he now understands and appreciates the right of appeal, but there is little doubt that in some cases he is inclined to abuse it and to exercise the right simply in an endeavour to escape justice which he knows is his due. Though he may not realise it, his hope rests mainly on the law of evidence. Section 301 of the Criminal Procedure Code, I consider, definitely tends to encourage such abuse. It is not easy to suggest how this tendency may be countered.

Increase of appeal fees seems at first sight an obvious solution. But a high flat rate for the Territory would prevent many genuine appellants appealing, unless exempted on grounds of poverty. A scale of fees for different areas based on a capacity to pay, as is the Hut and Poll Tax, might provide a solution. Remission on account of genuine poverty of the individual would of course still obtain anywhere.

8. Whilst the real criminal law of the Territory is generally understood—though evidence and procedure is not—statutory offences, e.g. pertaining to veterinary regulations, cotton uprooting, bhang etc., are frequently not, and, particularly amongst the older and more influential people, are merely regarded as an interference with private life, to be circumvented if possible.

9. The present procedure whereby a native having given evidence before a Subordinate Court has to appear again before the High Court is a great disability. Attendance before the lower Court may entail some few days absence from his home, but attendance before the High Court may entail some weeks' absence. This definitely makes them dislike appearing as witnesses with the result that important evidence is often not forthcoming. As an example, witnesses had to remain in the vicinity of the Sessions centre, two or three days journey from their homes, for a period of five to six weeks before their case came on and an acquittal resulted. This was during the cultivation season.

10. It is noted that not infrequently in cases of manslaughter, arson, rape etc. the sentence awarded by the High Court does not exceed that which could be awarded by a First Class Magistrate, and it would seem that such cases at least might be tried by the latter. All cases in which a sentence in excess of twelve months imprisonment is awarded are at present reviewed by the High Court. Subject to such review, the maximum sentence which a First Class Magistrate may award might be increased, so that all cases as far as possible may be tried in the Districts where they occur. The atmosphere of the District Court is far less awe inspiring to the native than the High Court, with consequent beneficial results as regards his evidence. The procedure of a preliminary enquiry for committal to the High Court involves practically as much work for the Magistrate as

a full trial and really only relieves him of the responsibility of giving judgment, which in cases of murder is admittedly considerable. If such procedure were adopted he should sit with native assessors in all serious cases. They can better appreciate the motives which may have actuated any party much more than a European, and for this reason are of definite value.

11.   Another disability which natives feel is the question of compensation. Under native law compensation always has been, and still is, of prime importance. A complainant, who has, say had a number of cattle stolen, though he may derive some satisfaction from seeing one at least of the offenders sentenced to imprisonment and probably a fine as well, does not consider justice has been done if he gets nothing on account of his lost cattle. The law permits of a part or whole of the fine being paid over to the complainant as compensation, but if the accused has no property of his own, or as frequently happens has successfully hidden it before hand, on which to distrain, the fine is not paid and complainant gets nothing. Native law provides for distraint on the family and in such a case it is obviously less likely that the family has no property or has succeeded in hiding all of it, though against this it may be said that frequently property is vested in any case in the family and not in the individual.

12.   I believe that the native realises that the main object of the Courts is justice and not punishment, but, for reasons which I have already stated, he fails to understand the full extent of justice. If an offender generally held in native opinion to be guilty is acquitted, it would seem fairly obvious that justice and not punishment is the main object, even though the justice is hard to understand.

13.   In short, it may be argued that the present law is too far in advance of the ordinary native capacity to understand and appreciate, and that if it were less so it would be more effective. Simpler law and better justice.

14.   I have endeavoured to show native opinion as I understand it. In conclusion, I would add that for the District Officer, whose duty it is to administer his District, maintain law and order and keep in touch with native thought and opinion as much as possible, a

simplification of the law would materially assist him in acquiring the greater confidence of, and understanding by, those to whom he is the local representative of Government. In mentioning this I would most emphatically state that it is not a basis on which my interpretation of native opinion is founded, but is merely ancillary thereto.

W. F. Page

A. W. WYATT

Installation of a Chief, Biharamulo District, 1932

Wyatt was born in 1900 and was educated at Leamington and Sandhurst. He served in the Hampshire Regiment and later in the King's African Rifles, from which he transferred in 1926 to the Tanganyika service. Wyatt's whole career was in the provincial administration. On retirement in 1949 he was acting provincial commissioner in the Central Province. He died in 1964.

This brief account of Chief Luginga's installation illustrates the continuance of traditional political institutions many decades after the arrival of European government.

Footnotes are Mr. Wyatt's.

Installation of a Chief, Biharamulo
District, 1932

. . . Chief Lugaga of Busambiro died on the 5th October, 1932. His son aged eight was chosen to succeed and the headmen and people were called together to recognise their new chief.

The old chief was buried with his ancestors on the 9th October. In the early morning the 10th the "Samulilo" (a) entered the vacant royal house and ignited a new fire with fire sticks. This was the fire of the new chief which burns through his life time. The old chief's fire had died out untended after his death. Members of the "batoni" (b) clans assembled and soon the new chief was borne in on the back

(a) The "Samulilo" is a hereditary office in one of the "batoni" clans. The holder is responsible for the chief's fire and has special duties concerning the chief's robing. He must remove the "vilungu" or badges of rank from a dead chief.

(b) The "batoni" form a group of six clans, some of slave origin, with duties about the chief's house. They keep the ceremonial robes emblems drums and stools in safe custody, as well as the secrets of the powerful "medicines" to some of which supernatural power is attributed, which have been collected by the various chiefs. They are taught the whereabouts of the

of the "Kiheka" (c), from a nearby hut. The new chief had not been allowed to enter the royal house since his father's death, nor had any of the tribal headmen (d).

The "Mzabura" (e) and Samulilo fastened a bracelet of small copper beads on the young chief's wrist and a white necklet about his neck. Then, together with the other "batoni", they squatted down, clapped their hands and gave the royal salute, "Kamerere Rugaba, Habuka Chambeka". One of the dead chief's wives was now brought in and chosen as the "wife" of the boy-chief, (she was a young woman). She was decorated with a lionskin necklace and a white "Kilungu" and began to cook and generally act as nurse to the chief. From now on the "batoni" surrounded the young chief and attended to his wants. They conversed with him on tribal matters and customs and the duties of a chief. Later in the day messengers were sent to call the people. The chief now took up his residence in the royal house, which is surmounted by an ostrich egg-shell and has two entrances, on the pattern of the ancient Sumbwa huto.

By the 12th October, nearly all the headmen and a great number of people had assembled in the open space near the chief's compound. The early comers had willingly joined some "batoni" in erecting a small hut of branches, more in the nature of a shelter than a dwelling. Another task was the setting up, suspended from a long pole, of a number of "ngoma" (drums), of a huge size. One of these called "Nyakasambiro" was only beaten on special days of great rejoicing. (f)

The young chief was awakened early by the "batoni" and anointed

---

royal graves and perform sacrifices at these on occasions. Some of them accompany the chief wherever he goes and are consulted by him on all matters. They choose and name the new chief. Their ancestors are supposed to have accompanied the original founder of the dynasty.

(c) Kaheka = to carry: Kisumbwa. A hereditary office but not in a "batoni" clan. The holder must carry a new chief until he has been placed on his "stool of state".

(d) The headmen are not allowed in the royal compound until the new chief is recognised for fear that one of them might seize the royal stool and proclaim himself chief.

(e) The Mzabura is a hereditary office. The holder is the senior of the "batoni" and leads the sacrificial ceremonies. He has great influence.

(f) Prior to this occasion the drum had last been beaten when the old chief returned from his journey to Dodoma in 1928 to meet H. R. H. the Prince of Wales.

on the head with oil before being clothed in a lion's skin, the skin of a young leopard and a baskcloth cape, of these the baskcloth cape was freshly made but the two skins were well worn and said to be those worn by the founder of the dynasty (circa 1750?). These are the chief's ceremonial garments. The royal emblems which were so noticeable a feature of his father's headdress may not be worn until a son is born to the chief. (g)

Soon after this, the boy chief was hoisted on to the back of the Kiheka and carried through the waiting crowds straight to the line of drums. Here the chief beat a roll on Nyakasambiro, (the vigour of which showed that he was not overcome by self-consciousness). No sooner had the chief given this signal than pandemonium broke loose from the hitherto comparatively silent crowd. Drums were beaten, dances commenced, guns were fired into the air and the royal salute frequently shouted.

Moving slowly through the rejoicing crowds, the chief was now carried to the small shelter and seated on one of the tribal stools. This stool was embellished by a number of powerful "medicines" tied about its legs. The "batoni" squatted round while the Mzabura stood by the chief's side and called to the headmen, "This is your chief, Lugina, (h) come and salute him." The headmen then squatted and gave the royal salute accompanied by numbers of their people. During the homage, the head of the Basingo clan approached the chief, (i) picked up an arrow which had been placed by his stool, turned and walked straight out of the crowd.

The chief remained for a considerable time, during which headmen and groups of people danced up to him, gave the royal salute and dispersed into the noisy crowd, singing and firing their guns. Finally, he was carried back to the royal house where he was divested of his robes and from which he appeared later in ordinary attire.

The crowd continued dancing and rejoicing until a late hour, while their boy chief moved freely among them, at times taking

(g) The son is not considered properly "born" until he can crawl.
(h) This is the first time the new chiefly cognomen had been pronounced publically.
(i) No members of the Singo clan are now allowed near the chief during his life time. If one is seen approaching he is asked from a distance what he desires and this is always given him. The chief may not set foot in their country. (This rule is waived under modern conditions).

a turn at the drums which seemed to have an especial attraction for him.

Thus was Matogoro bin Lugaga recognised by his people as Lugina III of Busambiro.

B. W. SAVORY

Safari Diary, Kigoma District, 1934

Savory was born in 1904 and educated at Oxford. He joined the Tanganyika service in 1927. Except for military service during World War II and brief assignments as a labor officer and as a magistrate he stayed in the mainstream of provincial administration throughout his career. He retired in 1957 after serving as provincial commissioner in the Western Province. At the time of this safari he was an assistant district officer based on the provincial headquarters at Tabora and temporarily posted to Kigoma District.

The most outstanding attribute of the good safari diary is its hour-by-hour account of the minutiae that officers thought about and dealt with on tours of inspection. Safaris lasting several weeks as this one did were microcosms of African life and colonial administration. Savory's assignment was to survey an undertoured area in connection with the campaign against sleeping sickness. He was to obtain accurate information as to which parts of the country were infested with tsetse flies and to investigate possibilities and problems of moving people to healthier places ("concentrations"). There was also the routine that all safaris covered: checking on the work of the native administration, and on demography, tax rolls, health, agriculture, justice, and communications.

These excerpts begin on 9 August 1934, when Savory and his party were at the village of Kamfwa's, i.e., the village whose chief or headman was called Kamfwa, just south of Uvinza on the Malagarasi River. The safari, about three hundred miles, was all on foot.

Footnotes have been added by the author to clarify various words and phrases used by Savory.

The map of the Kigoma District shown on the following page is based on an early touring map prepared by a Kigoma DO, C. H. B. Grant, during the 1920's. Grant's map was corrected and brought up to date by Savory on the safari described in this diary.

KIGOMA
UJIJI
Central Rail UVINZA Line
LAKE TANGANYIKA
MALAGARASI RIVER
Kamfwa's
Mlela's
Yabululu's
Kasanga
Pandashalo's
Bombwe
Lugufu
Kipehi's
Chambala's
Pandula
Malimungu's
Kasamia's
IKUSE MT.
Bilali's
Bujunja's
Kandege's
Matandiko's
Kamlala's
Sonaluse
Mitando's
Kabunsi's
Milala's
Pandajiwe's
NDURUMO MT.
Ngamia's
ITIASIO MT.

SAFARI ROUTE,
B. W. SAVORY,
TONGWE COUNTRY,
KIGOMA DISTRICT,
1934

0   10   20
MILES

. . . made circle to west of path to see what country was like, i.e. left Kamfwa's going northwest and returned from southwest when pram[1] read 19–20 miles. No fly encountered but said to be plentiful beyond in country bordering on Kwezi's.

Population denser than I expected. One finds groups of six huts in clearings of about 30 acres. These clearings have been gradually increased. In some cases one finds them abandoned. This seems to have driven the fly back. They are abandoned because soil gets exhausted or, I suspect, cursed. This mobility should be of use when concentration begins. . . . soil does not appear very rich; muhogo, matama, potatoes, maize cultivated.[2] Connection with Uvinza very strong. Saw only two children in 35 huts. Passed two small fires. In

1. Wheeled instrument for measuring distances.
2. Muhogo is cassava; matama (usually mtama) is millet or sorghum.

one place [there was] sign of anti-pig hedge . . . enclosing a large shamba.[3] Local natives appear . . . fairly fit.

One trouble over concentrations will be that huts are fairly substantially built . . . not merely grass rondevals as in Uha.

Returned at 16.00 hours to find Peter[4] had arrived. Checked his stores forthwith to be able to report breakages. They and microscope were in packing cases. Thank Heaven I brought tools. Contents O.K. but had to repack drugs for convenience in box Lockhart gave me. Shall return balance of what I had to dispensar at Uvinza. Am not sure what housing dispensar gets on safari. Finished at 17.30 hours.

Resulting delay fatal as Kahema had produced no posho.[5] It trickled in, with a negligible amount of beans, so, as it was getting late and porters had done nothing all day, I increased flour ration and was forced to cut beans out. A very bad start in a country where porters are so difficult to get. Have detailed Mbanda to leave for Mlela's at dawn, with instructions to have posho for 43 porters ready, and have asked Kahema to raise what beans he can before I leave tomorrow.

N.B. Simplest way of arranging posho: don't fiddle about with an inaccurate balance; say you want posho for x men, but that you want to see the people who bring it. Plank down x times ten cents to make it as easy as possible.

Thanks to having no decent neopara[6] [there has been] trouble over posho, delay over drugs . . . have so far been a glorified storekeeper and learnt little in the last two days. No food from 8.30 A.M. till 19.30 hours except three hard boiled eggs. Constant bogy of keeping porters hanging about idle, especially as have promised D.O. to try and do Tongwe in 19 days.

The shifting of population referred to above accounts for names of more non-existent places on map.

10th [Paulo] considers Watongwe will not kick much at concentrations as they are comparatively new arrivals and hence ancestors' graves are not of great importance. He thinks that the area we traversed yesterday could be considered as a concentration. I concur

---

3. Garden or plantation.
4. Native medical assistant or dispensar.
5. Ration of food.
6. (Usually mnyapara) head of porters on safari.

and prefer it to Nguruka as being nearer Uvinza, which is the accepted capital and also it is within tribal boundaries. The only question will be beehives, if Tongwe is free of sleeping sickness. However beehives can be put anywhere. The scattering of the Watongwe originates probably in fear of witchcraft and slave raiders (e.g. Angoni would not find the present Tongwe area a very profitable hunting ground). I cannot yet understand the way that in Kamfwa's area large spaces have been cultivated and then abandoned. I thought it was because the soil had become exhausted, but probably it is because inhabitants *think* . . . that soil is exhausted.

Query: In concentrations how much does one count on ground already clear and how much does one have to fell trees, a thing in which Watongwe are already versed?

Left Kamfwa's at 8.30 hours, pram reading 19.2; arrived Mlela's at 11.00, pram reading 25.9. A short safari in preparation for a long one to Yabululu's tomorrow. At mile 20.7 crossed Kambala River, dry at times. South side of this is a rocky face, and the path goes up a kind of cheddar Gorge. Pram moved with difficulty.

Mlela's consists of six huts. Met by some forty natives . . . the women threw matama at us (Omari says it is in imitation of Swahili rice throwing).

Peter got to work; was pleased to see there was no reticence in going to him. One cannot take a blood slide of an unsophisticated [native] who doesn't come for treatment, but I told him to take slides wherever possible. He missed his opportunity unfortunately.

Held a very informal baraza (snuff and cigarettes), but, Mlela being absent, and his wakili apparently half baked, did not sound the thirty natives present as to concentration. Assessment rolls extraordinarily accurate. Checked them over on P.C.'s system; in addition pretended at times not to know a native's father's name. When the name was given, as it was invariably, I knew my informants were acquainted with him.

Summary of Mlela's population:

Taxpayers	102		
Bachelors	34		
Married, childless	50	26	children
Married, 1 child	12	68	wives
" 2 children	24		
" 3 "	2		

Elsewhere total population is obtained by multiplying tax by three!

Posted receipt for microscope and drugs. Balance incomplete. Had to show Peter how it fits together.

Very cold even at midday. Yusuf down with fever. Shall give my Boys quinine regularly. Ali on duty but not too good.

Wrote to D.O. describing position and movements; sent letter by runner from Uvinza who brought maps and my private mail. Asked for syringes for Peter.

Peter's patients were:

Bronchitis	17	(not remarkable, considering
Ulcer	3	temperature)
Yaws	1	
Gonorrhoea	5	
	26	

Five blood slides only . . . all negative.

Did what I could to check assessment rolls. It seems very obvious that Watongwe will die out unless birth rate increases. This can be done only by eradicating sterility by putting them within hail of a hospital and placing them so that women are obtainable as wives and bachelors are in a position to raise mahari[7] of 50 to 100 shillings.

No fly seen on way. Bitten once in camp.

Water supply here excellent, permanent spring fifty yards from camp. This spring is the Sibimbisi shown on Burt's map.

Good banda[8] but used tent.

11th Yusuf and Ali unable to walk. Unwilling to split safari by leaving Peter behind with them, so had them carried in ground sheets. Left Mlela's 8.30; reached Yabululu's 15.30 hours. Pram reading 25.9 at start, 41.7 at finish, i.e. 15.8 miles. From mile 27 to 29.4 scrambled down gorge, very hard going; at mile 27 through grass through which pram would not pass.

Fly commenced at mile 33 and continued right to Yabululu's, where they occur in the village.

Welcomed with beans and maize instead of matama.

7. Bride price.
8. Shelter.

I should add that game is reported scarce on the way. Saw droppings of Roane and porcupine. Goats and dogs in village.

Two natives paid tax. One dear old gentleman had been lent his. Told Paulo to note him off for exemption next year. Tax seems to be a drill here: take your wax to Uvinza, get your four silver shillings and pay your tax. Hence when I was buying posho, nobody had the faintest idea of price. Eventually sat down and paid 4 cents per pint of flour, 2 cents per gill of beans ... i.e. one porter's ration. Porters seemed content and I hope it maintains Government prestige and encourages natives to see they get a fair price at dukas.[9]

... Yabululu's village is situated in a hollow; to the northeast is a long range of hills. Water supply is good. Saw first mango and banana trees.

12th Sunday, but not a day of rest and gladness. Yabululu seems fairly intelligent. Sounded him re concentration, then held a general baraza of the watwale.[10]

Mulalewa is dead and Saidi will replace him.[11] Kalengulula died in March, and Kasulamelemba two years ago, but have not been replaced because waraia can't agree, or perhaps because candidates can't pay necessary fees .... Ngawe is dead and candidate a child .... Yabululu has reigned since during the war. His father built present village.

I note that Mr. Tripe camped at Mulenga village. There was not a trace when I passed yesterday. Inhabitants are reported to have moved because ground was suitable for matama only and maize is liked.

Local inhabitants have heard of concentrations in Ufipa and elsewhere .... If they move of their own free will so easily ... a (government-sponsored) move won't be such a strain on them. Their attitude is, if the Serkali[12] orders us we will go, but ... a. Here we have space. What of our shambas. We are never at a loss for soil. Yabululu thinks his people are on the increase. I think [he has] the idea of heshima,[13] b. And more particularly, what of

9. Shops.
10. Headmen, usually between chief and village head.
11. These and following are heads of villages in the area.
12. Government.
13. Honor or respect.

our beehives, our sole source of cash for tax and clothing. By our custom we can only put beehives in our own [headmens' area], or when we die the question of inheriting the [hives] arises.

Also, consider the distance. Hives are heavy, and we like to go and put them somewhere close. Also . . . we have to put them up if a passing elephant has knocked them down.

Paulo . . . put my case well. I emphasized that concentration was not a trap to obtain tax but a means of insuring benefits [such] as medical attention, justice, etc. I let Yabululu and Company withdraw to discuss the idea, but they had nothing to add to the above two points, on which they, justifiably, feel very strongly.

Goats and some dogs here, latter measly. Goats cost 3 to 4 shillings and seldom breed. They are . . . obtained from Waha at Uvinza.

I am very puzzled about tax . . . astonished that so many pay here, as there is not the least compulsion to do so . . . .

An unfortunate thing has happened. Paulo says that D.O. has ordered that, now that tax has been reduced, some exemptees can now pay. Two greybeards came up with tax money, borrowed from able bodied relations, in one hand and exemption tickets in the other. I refused to take the money, or e'er long we shall be faced with the question when is an exemption ticket not an exemption ticket; tickets will fall into ill repute, and many bona fide cases will suffer.

I was very glad to find Paulo is preaching gospel of take your tax money yourself to the collector; don't entrust it to someone else . . . .

Peter has had a busy day. One double hernia cum elephantiasis gentleman seemed an interesting case. Gave him a warrant: Uvinza to Kigoma. Am trying to encourage locals to come for proper treatment. They certainly flock to Peter . . . .

Nine bloodslides taken, all negative except 1 sperillum.

[Beans] not cultivated much locally. Potatoes, mushrooms and wild vegetables seem a popular substitute. . . . Some anxiety seems to exist as to planting and harvesting during concentrating period.

Porter suffering from sperillum will leave for Uvinza tomorrow, or when his temperature falls, in charge of Uvinza katikiro[14] and one porter. To return blanket to akida there . . . .

14. Office messenger.

Starting at 8.45, reached Kipehi's at 3.00. Pram 41.7 at start, 56.3 on arrival. Ground very level. Passed deserted village of 8 well built huts 3 miles from Yabululu's. Inhabitants had moved for "agricultural" reasons. I still suspect magangas[15] are responsible, but Tongwe reticence plus conviction of a certain [headman] prevents hearing anything on this point.

I can't place Kipehi's on the map. We seemed to leave the main road at mile 49.7 and strike southeast, bearing left again at mile 52.6 where we went down hill till we reached Kipehi's. This village is situated on the Lugufu River which even at this season is some twenty feet wide. Lower down rice is cultivated.

Had to leave two loads at Yabululu's and he brought them along later with two porters . . . . [S]ince Peter's arrival, total is 44 (porters), not 42.

Yabululu is clearly very proud of his rolling acres and constantly refers to them, so will probably oppose concentration.

Kipehi is old but intelligent, understands my Swahili. Says this village was built the year the railway reached Tabora. He is a blacksmith and has just sold an axe for a cake of beeswax . . . .

One porter down with malaria. Cursed the day I ever engaged Watongwe. Am considering finishing up at Kamfwa's, say, where possibility of concentration could again be examined and discussed, and then getting more Waha. Several porters have coughs, yet Grant took the same tribe out in the rains without blankets! So far have had a casualty each day. Tripe safaried in October. Tomorrow, apparently, have a short safari to Mtwale Chambala's, 2 hours, but from there to Kasamia's is 7 hours according to Tripe's diary . . . .

More posho here than required, including maharage,[16] so bought from those who had come farthest; religiously weighed out pints of flour and gills of beans. I wonder whether this spot cash payment encourages them to bring posho in. Anyway, peaceful propaganda is the only way . . . if the Watongwe dig their toes in, it will require the whole K.A.R.[17] and Treasury to dislodge them.

Porter Shabani, Congolese, sick with malaria.

15. (Usually mganga) native doctor.
16. Beans.
17. King's African Rifles.

14th Shabani no better. Paid him wages and posho. Left supply of quinine. Arranged with Kipehi for him to stay in a room in a newly built house. Reluctantly compelled to take his blanket.

Arrived Chambala's at 9.45, having left at 8.30. Pram reading 56.3 and 60. Chambala's a typical Tongwe village, built in about 1909. Situated at foot of a hill. Mango trees and muhogo . . . practically all [Chambala's] people have paid tax. Four paid me in silver and asked for cents.

Peter reports that at Kipehi's and here natives very reticent about having bloodslides taken. Usual figures obtained for census . . . . [O]n entering village caught sight of Ikuse mountain, bearing 140 degrees. With native's help, placed it on map, where it is shown wrongly.

Not a sign of life between Kipehi's and Chambala's. Country flat. Trees high foliaged. Came down hill last ¾ mile . . . . [N]o fly en route, probably too early. Bitterly cold to midday.

Held "surprise" board on my cash:

Imprest shillings	400
Disbursements	49 – 27
Balance	350 – 73

(23 shillings; 186 half shillings; 141 – 73 cents)

15th Left Chambala's at 8.10, arrived Kasamia's 11.30. Pram start 60, finish 69.1. Tripe gives time of his journey as 6 hours. Even allowing for fact that Kasamia is in process of moving his village half a mile, can't understand it.

Shambas of former village have the strangest fence I've ever seen.

Fly commencing at mile 63.5 right up and into Kasamia's.

Old Chambala had widened path for about half a mile from his village. Usual nothingness on the way. Usual informal baraza here . . . .[18]

---

18. These demographic and health figures are given for each village along the way throughout the safari. Included in these excerpts are only two examples.

Taxpayers	86		
Bachelors	26		
Married, childless	30	Boys	39
" 4 children	6	Girls	28
" 3 "	6		
" 2 "	8		
" 1 child	10		

Peter's patients have been:

. . . Bronchitis	7
Flu	4
Headache	7
Yaws	4
Ulcer	1
Paralysis	1
. . .	
Roundworm	2
Colic	1

In evening saw Kasamia . . . and elders re concentrations. The village, ½ mile away, which they are evacuating because soil is exhausted, has a wonderful pig-proof fence. The new village has a layout which would do credit to a surveyor; rope must have been used for it.

They profess themselves willing to move but raise usual objections . . . . [A]sked to be moved to somewhere in Tongwe but fear displeasure of mwami[19] in whose land they are placed . . . .

Kasamia claims he and his former village were here when the Germans came . . . .

I hold that concentrations want nursing at first. It will be easier for visiting administrative officers and Paulo to do so at Uvinza than having to make special visits to Nguruka [the projected concentration area]. Paulo suggests eastern Tongwe, who are adjacent, might be put up at Nguruka. If we interfere with beekeeping we are asking for trouble . . . .

16th   Left Kasamia's at 8.10, arrived at Bujunja's at 11.45. Pram 69.1 . . . 78.7. At mile 78.4 struck southeast. At mile 74 road

19. Chief.

forks . . . left to Bugwe. At mile 76.1 crossed Mufizi River, tributary of Lugufu . . . .

Bujunja, who appears not all there, is engaged in moving his village from site used since German times . . . fly from mile 73 onwards and thick in village. Some dogs and goats.

Usual statistics obtained . . . interrupted by old gentleman asking for salt. Rations flocked in . . . runner arrived with letter from Maclean and Court forms from D.O. Also private mail . . . .

17th Decided not to march today till definite news of route, water and supplies on road to Matale obtained. Wrote S.S.O.[20] acknowledging receipt of instructions, which will be difficult to follow. Wrote D.O. re rations. Runner, a Uvinza sanitation labourer who had come from there, sleeping twice en route, left at 1.45.

Trouble again with Watongwe porters who think they are going a three months safari.

Shall have to sleep in the bush on the way to Matale.

. . . Saw zebra but bagged nothing.

Checked posho. Reserve we are carrying will suffice 4½ days. No fly seen all day.

18th Left Bujunja's 8.05. Pram 78.7. Arrived 14.15 at Kakomo River. Pram 93.1. At mile 83.9 passed Limusana village . . . tobacco and muhogo doing well. Eight huts. At mile 86.7 crossed Bulamata Matale border, Mgondosi River, permanent river running north. At mile 92 crossed road with bearing of 195 degrees leading to Bushamba. Camped in bush. Some flour brought from Bujunja's, rest issued from reserve. Beans also. Simba[21] unable to go out (had seen signs of roane and impalla) owing to malaria. Peter reports couch mixture finished. Good thing I brought it.

19th Simba running temperature of 101. Unable to walk owing to purges. Fortunately bringers of flour yesterday had not left; so made [litter] in which they carried him. Cold last night intense. Glad I didn't camp nearer river.

---

20. Sleeping sickness officer.
21. Hunter whose job it is to supply party with game; game scout.

Above delayed start. Started at 8.30. Pram 93.1. At 96.4 passed Malimba village, six huts in Ubende palisade style and stockade of 600 yards circumference there. Area reported clear of fly. Good crop of muhogo and tobacco . . . . Ujiji tobacconists come here to buy. As to beeswax the two annual harvests from some 60 hives may yield anything from 3 to 15 cakes.

Heard at village that it was 8 hours to Ubende and that Mwami there was absent. Reluctantly compelled to cut Ubende out. Going with Simba difficult, so decided to head for Kabunsi's. If rations are adequate shall go from there to Ngondo.

After leaving Malimba, going became appalling, a series of steep hills with bushy paths . . . through which pram would hardly pass.

Kabunsi's village has 4 huts and was built in Belgian times. Careful enquiries here convince me that Ubende and Ngondo on Burt's map should be to the southwest. Corrected Kabunsi's north border on it.

Saw fourth case of neck goitre in three villages. Natives think it due to drinking bad water.

Hear Ngondo and Ubende not too good for beeswax, so [they] cultivate rice in Bilali's [on Lake Tanganyika], where Arabs buy. Arabs used to buy anyway from Uvinza, but now natives find it more profitable to take their wax to Uvinza.

No fly reported in Matale, but Matete said to be stiff with it . . . . [Z]ebra, roans, buffalo and wildebeast reported locally. Saw some Kwale and birds that looked like cockatills, also some swallows.

. . . [T]he whole trouble about this part of the world is the uncertainty of getting posho, or, if one issues one's reserve, of replacing it. 43 porters are rather a swarm. Have decided definitely to go right into Uvinza to refresh imprest, obtain cents, stores, more Waha,[22] if powers [his superiors] agree. I feel the days involved will be justified by the result. At present most of my time seems to be spent over commissariat.

20th Left Kabunsi's 8.15. Pram 101.3. Arrived Ngondo 11.30, pram 110.1 . . . Mitando's, 13 huts, is one of the oldest villages in

22. The Ha people, from north of Uvinza, were hardier and in general more enterprising and dependable than the Watongwe, through whose country this safari is moving and who have supplied most of the porters.

Tongwe, and is encircled by a ditch for defense purposes. It has the highest manyara trees I have seen.

N.B. Kabunsi was not paid his salary last year.

He boasts his area is free of fly, but [we] encountered it at mile 102.5 and heavily at Luegele River, his boundary with Ngondo.

Decided to stay here tomorrow and make a day visit to Ubende. Bought flour accordingly, baksheeshing[23] a little salt to those whose flour I did not need. This marketing a long process. One woman brought in a small basin of excellent groundnuts. Runner arrived from Uvinza . . . with mail, exemption certificates, arms licenses and syringe, but no distilled water.

Inspected local crops. Potatoes a washout because of elephant. Maize has done fairly well and tobacco promises excellently.

Seven goats, ex Buha, and usual pi dogs, also doing well.

Saw zebra spoor for first time this safari.

Local inhabitants do not fence but put towers . . . for pig scaring. No baboon here.

Luegele River is a good water supply. It . . . enters [Lake] Tanganyika in Bulimba apparently.

Am commencing a separate book for Peter so shall not refer to him further here.

This country again has hills inaccessible to porters, so time is lost zigzagging along valleys. Three more cases of neck goitre. Hear it is common in Ubende. One woman claims to have been cured by a series of small incisions in the neck. Apparently quite small children develop it.

21st Left for Ubende with Paulo at 9.00. Pram 110.1 . . . . [A]rrived at Sonaluse 11.30. pram 114.1 . . . . [T]elegraph line passes one mile west of Mitando's, so map is fairly accurate . . . .

The road to Mitando's goes along the Luegele River valley, and one crosses the river just before reaching the village.

Village has eight huts and is well laid out . . . fly the whole way, in small non-biting numbers, but worse at Ngondo camp. Saw fresh buffalo spoor en route; otters said to exist in river. Saw small fish.

---

23. Baksheesh is a gratuity or tip.

As at Kabunsi's: 1. explained the danger of sending tax money by deputy; have received about half the taxes . . . that way, 2. objects of concentrations . . . census work done.

. . . Returned to Ngondo and held baraza at 16.00 hours . . . .

Procedure is as follows: ask people . . . whether they are increasing or decreasing. They will always say they are decreasing . . . make this an excuse for census work. Then lead up to concentrations. Usual nervousness about beehives and crops . . . average hives here 40 per man I should say.

N.B. Local mtwale ascribes low birth rate to . . . poison, extract of crocodile administered to children by enemies . . . .

[The people] say they gave [a local tax official] their tax moneys two months ago to take to Uvinza and haven't seen him or their tickets since.

I hear the true mwami here was put to school[24] and [a wakili] appointed in his absence . . . has continued . . . ever since, the true mwami fearing to return.

. . . [P]orters repaired "drawbridge" into Ngondo village.

Assessment rolls for Ngondo and Ubende leave much to be desired, though, in view of the scattered "villages," one can't altogether blame the hutcounter concerned.

Taxpaying complex probably due to legions of petty headmen who wish to justify their existence.

22nd Tongwe porter . . . reported sick and unable to walk. Symptoms vague but suggested spleen or rheumatism. On enquiry found that he had often suffered from this complaint. Peter thinks a rest cure necessary. Left Uvinza Katikiro to see him to his home in Yabululu's (could find no other reliable person to send) . . . .

Left Simba, who is now pronounced fit, to deal with Mitando's elephants. He whined for salt.

Left Mitando's 8.20. Pram 118.1. Arrived Majegwe at 10.00 hours, mile 123.1. Poisonous country, grass everywhere. Guide, who appears to be . . . village idiot, announcing [that we had taken a wrong turn and] wasted a day . . . typical of this area; . . . nobody knows the roads outside his unit.

Pandajiwe (headman of nearby village) is deaf and not far re-

24. I.e., that he had been sent to a school for chiefs run by the government.

moved from the congenital idiot. Kasagula is a rival mwami whom many accept because P. is infirm and old. Early [in] 1933 Kasagula came to Boma[25] and asked to be made mwami but was shot out by R-J.[26]

Hope D.O. won't kick at our delay . . . it's the remotest parts which require most attention . . . and will be the most difficult to concentrate.

Usual interview with Pandajiwe and his subjects, seven in number. His version is that Kasagula took a false report of his (P's) death to the Boma . . . anyway the assessment roll bears his name. An example of how much the unfortunate D.O. knows about this part of the world.

Usual story: population decreasing. Paulo and Omari think this is an exaggeration, merely to give an impression of former prestige. I have been very struck by the absence of greybeards. Are they dead or hiding?

. . . [O]ne must consider the younger . . . Swahili speaking [native] . . . his journeys to Uvinza must make him rather sophisticated.

Read Tripe's report. He points out that early traders moved [from] Bagamoyo [on the Indian Ocean] to Ujiji [on Lake Tanganyika] and the Watongwe met them at Uvinza.

Peter reports that local women would not come to him as he had no incantations. Compare this with Ngondo account of low birth rate and one finds that South Tongwe and North Tongwe are two different places.

Omari's account of the [bride price] is that the 200 shillings idea is rubbish. Father-in-law allows his daughters to be married on the hire purchase system, and the initial payment is a small one. When father-in-law feels hungry or thirsty he presses for an instalment. Presumably father-in-law always selects sons-in-law likely to pay up. The process of disintegration has undermined the clan system which limited the choice of females originally.

Checked cash and found 60 cents short. Made good. Hope P.C. is not under impression I am changing porters at every village. Anyway porters have to receive posho when paid off, so not much economy results.

25. Fort originally, now administrative headquarters.
26. Initials of the district officer at Kigoma, under whose authority this safari is being conducted.

Have decided to ask D.O. for leave to employ 30 Waha permanently....

P.C.'s ... instructions are not to leave Tongwe till I am sure all is well, hence, after recent discoveries, I feel bound to visit every area ....

23rd Left Pandajiwe's at 8.00. Pram 123.1. Arrived Milala's 3.30. Pram 139.4. A somewhat bloody march. Started in thick elephant grass, then along a valley of charred trees and rocks. At 11.50 struck Kasagula's at mile 132.5. A village almost as bad as Pandajiwe's but built lately. Decided to push on, as ... Milala is expecting us [and] local food and water ... don't look too promising ... [C]ouldn't get much news as to route and time. Locals suggested a route which would avoid Bushamba, but [I] didn't want to let Milala down, so proceeded. No water en route and porters dislike carrying it in gourds. Got fresh guide at Kasagula's and paid off village idiot.

Crossed a parched and arid waste, crossing boundary into Bushamba, a dry river bed, at mile 134.7. Half a dozen huts just before it, occupied but nobody about. A long scramble up the last range of hills and down the other side into Milala's. Everything clean, and plenty of posho ready. Issued it at once and saw [that] porters had plenty of firewood.

Women afraid to go to Peter. Milala says leopards are hard on his goats, but three [leopards] have been shot .... [E]xcellent little rest camp and kitchen ready.

Milala in spotless kanzu.[27]

Long talk with Paulo. Said I would write from Bugwe to D.O. explaining that though Paulo's work is piling up at Uvinza his presence brings home to local [people] that Uvinza is the capital; Paulo holds that Ubende plaintiffs must sue Uvinza defendants at Uvinza [and] suggests that Watongwe keep away in the bush as they fear being called out as porters. He volunteered the suggestion that I must increase Waha [porters] at Uvinza. Local N.A.s[28] incapable of providing porters.

When marking up journey on chart tried to calculate how far it

27. Nightgown-like garment, the usual Swahili dress.
28. Native authorities, local chiefs recognized by government.

will be to Uvinza; it seems at least 120 miles, and at earliest we shall arrive on September 5th. If we can visit every "Chiefdom", it will probably be the first time this has ever been done in a single safari. Hope our efforts are justified by the result.

24th   My intention yesterday was to leave late this morning so as to give Peter a chance to do his stuff, Paulo a chance to fraternize with Milala and Milala a chance to meet me.

When definite information was received, found march to [next village] was a stiff one, so decided to let porters rest. Wrote private mail and also to Medical Officer re drugs, and to D.O. re porters and route. Got [information on tsetse] flies up to date.

Was pleased to see Paulo and Milala sitting cheek by jowl over a civil case. Had to pull up ex Katikiro Abedi (I hear he was an askari[29] but was sacked for assaulting an N.C.O.) for not saluting them.

Could not see Milala till after dinner when he came along. With pleasing frankness he is dead against concentrations. They will accentuate V.D. infection and ruin beeswax producing. I was interested to hear that a fair amount of the wax goes over the border. This may support my theory that Ubende ought to be under Tabora District, concentrations being on the border, and therefore easier of access by road than from Kigoma. Wabende need not be pulled out of Ukabende then, as would be the case if they were put south of Buholoholo.

Paulo has very wisely let Kasagula vs. Pandajiwe matter slide. Whichever man is put in, the supporters of the other will clear out, just when we don't want them to . . . .

25th   Left Milala's at 7.45. Pram 139.4. Arrived Ngamia's at 14.45, pram 152. Going was worse than on 23rd as we had to climb Ndurumo Mountain. This has a bearing of 160 degrees on Itiasio Mountain (6,100 feet, according to the map) which . . . is not very much higher . . . owing to intervening mountain range, we have had to make a long detour to the south to reach Bugwe from Matete.

At Bugwe met Andrew and Takadiri. Took over a completed and part completed book of [tax] tickets . . . with cash collected. 620

29. Soldier.

shillings. Fortunately it included some copper. They report a great exodus northwards to sell beeswax, through an Indian, [name] unknown, has an itinerant trader's licence in East Tongwe, and is paying two shillings a cake. Issued Andrew two tax books. Rather tickled to find locals were tapika-ing[30] hard, to see that our visit brought no untoward results.

Have made rule that [wood] must be stacked for night fires before posho is issued.

Gave Andrew some of my cartridges. Consider he needs self protection.

I feel we take the hutcounters' work too much for granted. This is not good country to safari in, and our native clerks stroll round, usually without an escort, and collect thousands of shillings at [a salary of] 40 shillings a month. I agree with Kitching, who always marvelled so little tax money was lost.

26th   Left Ngamia's 7.50. Arrived Kamlala's 16.15 . . . . Pram start 152, finish 168. Leopard seen en route. Poisonous country, but porters never groused . . . . As tent was pitched issued snuff and cigarettes. Medical inspection. Plenty of posho available.

So hilly and circuitous was the route that compass bearings were very difficult. Possibly because I'm not allowing for magnetic variation, map seems to show Bugwe too far north.

Bushamba Bugwe border at mile 163.4. At mile 162.1 struck the first flat, open space I've seen [in this area], about ¾ [of a mile] diameter, a natural landing ground. At 165.6 descended into Kamlala's. End of Itiasio range I hope as my heavy rubber shoes are worn out and my light ones nearly so.

Saw first guinea fowl and a regular jabbercock of a bird; but it takes five minutes to unpack my gun. Shall remedy this when loads are combed out.

No fly seen all day.

. . . Simba here. Had drawn a blank on the shamba raiders.

I'm the first European here for ten years . . . .

Two watwale have one man each. What a dreadful thing a revolution would be . . . .

30. Paying up; literally, vomiting.

28th   Left Kamlala's 8.25, arrived Matandiko's 14.00, pram 168 start, 179.8 at finish. On march noticed ... porter ... not looking too good. Had him relieved of his load. On reaching camp his temperature was 104.5. Had hut built and gave him aspirin and hot honey and milk . . . .

This village . . . is heavily stockaded. The farther south one gets the heavier the stockades, except in villages big enough to defend themselves, e.g. Milala's and Kamlala's.

This is the worst village I've struck for fly. Six huts and very dirty. Yet Ngulukimba at mile 176.2 was spotless, the former built in Belgian times, the latter two years ago.

29th   Left at 8.15, arrived at 14.00, Kandege's. Pram 179.8 at start, 192 at finish. First three miles along broad valley lousy with fly. Encountered undulating hills as in North Tongwe.

Kandege doesn't look much but has brains ... he claims his father settled here just after the Angoni invasion. Last European here [was] the Bwana with the gold teeth, "five years ago." Checking this over I found it was Grant in 1924!

. . . An Indian, Bwana Chenja . . . has come here to buy beeswax. Although his price is lower and natives sell to him rather than go to Uvinza . . . his presence probably encourages beekeeping locally . . . .

Kandege is the first chief to realize what sleeping sickness means; he came off his own bat to have a bloodslide taken, as he had stopped several tsetse . . . .

Speaking generally, there seems much more movement here in the southeast than elsewhere, to and from Ubende and Tabora . . . .

An unpleasant incident in the evening. Waha and Watongwe started scrapping over cooking pots. Fearing it might spread I sailed in and scattered all parties. Later took them to Kandege [to] apologize and did not allow ngama[31] in evening.

Peter running temperature ... Kandege had had a banda built here [I rewarded with salt] so put latter in there and a Tongwe whom I found coughing when I made usual round to see fires stoked last thing.

31. Dance.

At a guess we have 90 miles more to go but I fear we shan't be in Uvinza before 8th as chiefs' villages require two nights.

30th　Peter's temperature 100.2 degrees and porter's 99.

Inspected assessment rolls. Of 20 who paid yesterday I can place only 6, three of whom I have inserted . . . . [H]utcounters have not been walking around but getting hearsay evidence from [native officials] . . . ten percent will have to be added to my census totals, though proportions will remain unchanged . . . married to bachelors, etc.

Shentsi Khan, Indian trader, called. His operating base is Sindwi, 6 hours from here, and his duka at Uruwira, I gather . . . .

31st　Left Kandege's 8.15. Pram 192. Arrived Malimungu's 15.30. Pram 208.9. Malimungu does not actually live at Kilossa (his village) but turned up there P.D.Q. Kilossa has only 7 huts now, but judging by manyara hedges, one at least is old. Road level and winding. Vultures and eagles in evidence . . . tsetse everywhere. Noticed that very few people turned out to receive us. Paulo says Malimungu is unpopular because he has withdrawn into the bush with his wives (don't blame him!). There is a story that in Belgian times M's predecessor was imprisoned for killing a man . . . and was starved to death by a warden bribed by M's partisans. I noticed that the builders of my kitchen vanished as soon as the work was finished. Water supply poor. A lot of natives reported to be fishing . . . saw some nets, rather like a snow shoe only smaller . . . .

Careful to pay for all work done, to show there is no forced labor nowadays.

September 1st　At Malimungu's 42 natives turned up to baraza. Assessment rolls checked. Usual chaos. Usual attitude to concentrations . . . .

In epidemiological work have noticed a complete absence of "flappers." I think they are booked at an early age to prevent someone else snapping them up, so are described as adult and married; a large number of middle aged and oldish men with infant children; a very small number of greybeards . . . .

2nd Left Malimungu's 8.15, pram 208.9. Arrived Pandashalo's 14.50, pram 223.2.

. . . On arrival asked for bearings and feel I have marked map fairly accurately; I was badly out at Kilossa . . . .

Checked tax money. Correct. Shillings 432 so far, all unasked for . . . .

We were accorded a right royal welcome by lasses and lads of village.

Pandashalo had kitchen and banda and hospital all ready . . . .

Marked slides as Peter has run out of stain.

3rd Commenced forestry enquiries amongst Watongwe porters, hoping they would be more in a position to know whole of Tongwe; have intentionally deferred doing so, so as to get a fair average of whole area. Results discouraging. Tendency to go for trees of exemptional interest, e.g. mninga, which has been seen twice only, so far . . . .

Simba shot a buffalo . . . .

Told all present that they should bring their shauris[32] to Uvinza and warned them of the danger of detailing others to pay their tax for them . . . .

4th Decided to remain here so that I can embark on other sections [of the safari report] and get it in to D.O. soon after reaching Uvinza. . . .

Further specimens of new fly caught. On the whole, flies are most active from 16.00 hours till dusk.

Porters had an ngama in evening. Issued no beans as they have a balance of meat from yesterday.

5th Left Pandasholo's 8.15. Pram 223.3. Arrived at hut of Mtwale Kajembe's at 2.30, pram 235.9.

. . . [C]amped in a gap between two ranges. Two huts at mile 228.7. Got water, and runner from Bombwe brought mail. Nothing from D.O. save note . . . about returning quickly.

. . . In evening tried to measure shambas but decided not to as sole

32. Affairs, discussions, plans. Also complaints made to officials.

inhabitant, age about 70, had received extensive help from his sons in law and results would therefore be misleading. . . . [F]ly thick from mile 232.5 onwards.

6th   Left Kajembe's 8.25, delay due to rain and assessment rolls. Pram 235.9. Reached Pandula, a village in . . . Makokoto's area, at 15.30. Pram 248.5. Passed between two mountains and began rising gradually. Crossed three dry water courses. Thick vegetation and steep sides made first one dangerous going. Arrived at Kamtana's village, an 8 hut affair, spread over the valley. Simba gave out there. Tummy trouble. So got 4 porters and made a [litter]. Immediately afterwards started a very steep climb . . . a mile brought us to level ground and we continued, zigzagging all over the place, to Pandula, an attractive little village with extensive muhogo plantations and good water, fuel and posho supplies. . . .

I believe a hutcounter was sent here in February of this year, in which case he seems to have skipped this village completely. . . .

Am not at all certain where we are, but make it, as the crow flies, about 16 miles southeast of Bombwe . . . sick porter's temperature 100 degrees in evening . . . three bronchitis cases. . . .

No food till dinner time and on duty till 7.00, so a trifle tired.

7th   Left Pandula 8.00 hours. Pram 248.5. Arrived Lugufu 12.15 hours. Pram 259.4.

. . . Sangama's temperature normal. No honey obtainable to give him home made cough cure.

. . . saw two canoes on the river which was very low.

. . . there are not sufficient locust-proof crops here . . . [for] concentrations must get . . . potatoe vines which mature quickly. Rather hard luck on the natives if they plant muhogo and are [moved] before reaping it.

Bad headache but no temperature. . . .

8th   Left Lugufu 8.30. Pram 259.4. Arrived Bombwe 11.45. Pram 267.

. . . [D]ecided to send [porter] Sangama home as he lives 8 hours away . . . his temperature has been normal 48 hours . . . paid off porter Alimasi, who comes from same village, to see him home. . . .

I don't think Alimasi was altogether malingering, but he dashed off the minute he was paid, like a long dog.

Hardly any fly en route. Country varied from a visibility of 200 yards to dense thickets. . . .

Good view of Ikuse [mountain] at Lugufu on bearing of 259.4.

9th Bombwe is too important a center to rush through, so stayed here today. Worked on census, for what my figures are worth, as these soloist spokesmen have often not the faintest idea of what they are saying.

Packed trees for sleeping sickness officer. . . .

Wrote to D.O. informing him I hope to reach Uvinza on the 14th and that I hope to get drugs from Medical Officer . . . there. . . .

10th Ali set kitchen alight. Fortunately wind [was] in right direction or tent would have followed. . . . Total losses: two tins of ointment.

. . . [C]ouldn't start till 8.45. Pram 267. Reached Kasanga 14.45. Pram 280. Am hopelessly out on map. . . .

At mile 276.8 commenced climbing Kabumbu hill and eventually rose to 5980 feet. Flat dry mbuga on top. Dropped down to Kasanga 5610 feet.

Find I wronged hutcounter. He did go to Lugufu, but he certainly never came here. Koi, who is a live wire, is gazetted as a mtwale in P.C.'s list. . . .

Asked Koi for census information. The little he gave me was reliable but contradicted what the [headman] at Mlela's told me.

[Another official] wishes to sue Yabululu for extorting two goats from him on false charge of adultery. Thought it best for Paulo to issue [complaint forms] at once, as have been very suspicious at lack of complaints and think this may encourage [victims] to come forward. . . .

One Arab and one Indian trader here; no time to interview them . . . no time for food from 8.00 a.m. to 8.00 p.m.

Very cold; thermometer 56 degrees at 22.00 hours. . . .

J. F. R. HILL, c.m.g.

Annual Report on Native Affairs, Rungwe District, 1940

Hill was born in 1905 and educated at Oxford. He joined the Tanganyika service in 1928, serving in a wide variety of districts and becoming a provincial commissioner after World War II. In the early 1950s he served as member of the Executive Council for communications, works and development planning and later as chairman of the Tanganyika Broadcasting Corporation. After retirement in 1957 he undertook special assignments in the Bahamas and in Zanzibar.

This report was prepared when Hill was in charge of Rungwe in the Southern Highlands early in World War II. It has a pungency and directness that were characteristic of many officers who believed economic development to be essential, even if it involved a watering down of traditional cultures. Of special interest is the contrast between changes brought on by voluntary native support for the war effort and the continuing hold of tradition, e.g., reluctance of tribesmen to accept rinderpest vaccination for their cattle.

Annual Report on Native Affairs, Rungwe District, 1940

. . . After the outbreak of war in September, 1939, and the gradual adjustment from the immediate excitement to the first few months, the natives of Rungwe by and large returned to normality in 1940. Indeed the people were little affected by the war during the early part of the year. Very few were serving in the armed forces. Enemy European population had been effectively dealt with, and although some were inclined to be grim owing to the inevitable rise in the price of cloth, hoes and other commodities, yet the vast majority remained gay, indulging with their wonted energy in litigation, searching for work on the Lupa [gold field in neighboring district] and cultivating steadily if not impressively. Wild rumour at times disturbed their peace of mind. Chiefs however and people alike were constantly warned to turn deaf ears to travellers tales, and indeed the avidity with which "Habari za Vita" was sought proves that reliance was great on the word of Government. Nevertheless rumour is a dangerous jade especially among the sharp witted Wanyakyusa among whom if she obtained a footing would be difficult to dislodge.

The undoubted loyalty of the Chiefs and people has been proved in several ways. The only objection to the proposed loan from the Native Treasury to His Majesty's Government and Tanganyika Government was that an outright gift had not been suggested to them. Spontaneous contributions to War Funds from natives have amounted to over Shs. 1,500/– representing gifts small and large from all sections of the native community. Over 60 volunteers for the King's African Rifles came forward when the news was spread in November that men were required. Not least were the efforts made by the Native Authorities in obtaining men for the East African Military Labour Corps from October onwards. Many were sent but few were chosen, for although the quotas were fulfilled by all the chiefs save one, the first batches were very uneven, numbering many who were obvious rejects on the score of age as well as unfitness. Later the conscripts (for such they were with the exception of perhaps 5% volunteers) were of a better type. The Native Authorities send in a most reluctant body of men, but this reluctance lessens after a few days in camp, until at the time of dispatch they leave singing and cheering. One man in fact who was left behind from a batch, because he required further treatment before he was passed fit, wailed his sorrow aloud before the assembled crowd! The desertions were remarkably few, apart from the men of Bundali who absconded in considerable numbers. Some of these have been brought to book.

The work involved in the housing, feeding and clothing and organzing these recruits at Tukuyu was heavy. The Medical Department are in particular to be thanked for their cooperation and indefatigable work in examining these men.

The following figures are of interest:

1. Labour Corps.
    (a) Number of men sent in by Native Authorities   1195
    (b) Rejects as unfit   763
    (c) Deserted   58
    (d) Accepted   374
    (e) Actually dispatched   365
2. King's African Rifles Volunteers.
    (a) Accepted since 1st January, 1940   129
    (b) Dispatched   109
3. East African Medical Services.
    (a) Accepted   22
    (b) Dispatched   16
4. Others. Drivers, etc.
    Dispatched   6
5. Number who have left the District for military work
        during 1940.
    1. East Africa Military Labour Corps   365
    2. King's African Rifles before October   66
                     Since October   43
    3. Medical Services   16
    4. Others   6

                               Total   496

This may seem a small loss of manpower considering the population of some 52,000 males, but it must be remembered that such absentees, unlike the temporary emigrants to the Lupa, will be absent for a long period from a district where nearly all the cultivation is done by males. Saturation point in the manpower available is less than in most districts.

There have been no major changes in the personnel of the Native Authorities during the year. Politically the district has remained quiet, indeed singularly free from the disturbing element of the internal political quarrels, which so frequently, owing to the structure of the Native Authorities, arise. Traditional claims to independence, so often justified in tribal eyes, inevitably produce heart burning among those who cannot owing to their numbers above all be recognized as independent chiefs, but are of necessity relegated to being headmen of minor importance in the Native Authority structure. Acceptance of the present tribal structure and obedience to the recognized chiefs is growing year by year. Boundary disputes are common every year and 1940 proved no exception. Most of these have been settled though whatever decision is made, they are liable to spasmodic eruption.

It has been proposed that Headman Kasambala be recognized as a Chief, since his area and the population under his control make his present position somewhat anomalous. It is hoped that this proposal will be acceptable for the increased authority he will obtain will stabilize the Masebe court and his area.

The separatist tendencies of the Kiwira Court have not lessened: indeed these will probably increase until the death of the old Chief Mwangoka of Katumba, when the heir apparent, who is a strong character may be able to check this unjustified ambition on the part of the Kiwira Headmen.

In Lusungo where the eldest son of the aged Chief Mwakabulufu has been disinherited and now resides in H.M. Prison, the son of the second house Mwakafwila was accepted to act as Regent. He has performed his duties with steadiness and reliability even if his qualities as a leader are not outstanding.

Some of the weaker vessels notably Msomba of Bundali and Mwankuga of Itagata have shown no improvement. Both got into trouble, the former about recruiting, while the latter showed his lack of control over his people during the rinderpest campaign.

The two full meetings of the Council of Chiefs, which take place every year are tending to become more truly representative of native opinion. Indeed the council appears to be growing in the confidence and ability to tackle matters concerning them all in plenary session. Nevertheless individual dissenting voices are often raised. This was instanced when the question was raised of the liability to pay damages by the owners of cattle which trespassed. Such violent disagreement resulted that the proposal had to be temporarily shelved. Many matters of interest are discussed including of course the Native Treasury Estimates. While the discussions on these are not marked by any real financial understanding, yet there is an increasing realisation that any monies received or expended should be in their ultimate control. Judicially the Council has shown itself wise: its jurisdiction in certain original cases, having been approved towards the end of 1939, has proved of considerable value.

"Business as usual" in the Rungwe Native Courts connotes strenuous and almost daily work for the Chief, Elders and clerk. Not only are the cases in themselves numerous, but the method of hearing through an advisor or advocate, and the amount of irrelevant evidence that is heard lengthen the process. Moreover much time is taken up—and quite rightly—with the issuing of process and enforcement of judgments. There is still much room for improvement in these two matters. Cases are on the whole judged and recorded well. Indeed many of the numerous appeals are brought somewhat optimistically on very slender grounds. The fees are no deterrent even to the frivolous appellant. Nevertheless the majority of appeals are well founded as is shown by the fact that of 631 appeals brought to the Native Appeal Court 267 were allowed. This proportion of 42% successful appeals was as high in appeals to the District Commissioner for out of 133 appellants, 50 succeeded in winning their cases. There were 12 appeals laid to the court of the Provincial Commissioner during the year.

The total number of cases heard in the lower courts was nearly 6000. The vast majority of these were civil suits, mainly for dowry and adultery.

Soil erosion offences accounted for the majority of cases taken under section 8 of the Native Authority Ordinance.

The court books have been inspected regularly and in support of the claim that substantial justice is regular and constant, only 8 judgments have been revised by the District Commissioner.

The treasury remains in a very healthy state at the end of the year. In spite of the shortfall in rebate on tax (some £400), the revenue from Court Fees fully makes up this deficit by showing an increase of about £450 on the estimated figure. The following buildings have been constructed during the year:

1. Chiefs camp at Mpuguso (partially completed)
2. A new court house at Malangali
3. A new dispensary at Malangali
4. New wing and staff houses at Mpuguso School
5. A footbridge over the Luswiswi River
   (partially completed)

A proposal to loan £3000 to His Majesty's Government and the Tanganyika Government is under consideration.

The books of account have been carefully and tidily kept. Collections of Native House and Poll Tax have been disappointing. The district is now assessed with a high degree of accuracy, but continued emigration to Mbeya though it seems on a decreasing scale, has somewhat further reduced the number of potential taxpayers. Poor rice crops, a shortfall, in the reapings of Native Coffee and more particularly recruiting for the East African Military Labour Corps. The efforts towards the end which generally have a marked stimulus on collections have been partially nullified this year, for not only have the chiefs and headmen had a busy time gathering their quota of conscripts, but many have undoubtedly avoided tax barazas for fear of being drafted to the labour corps.

Comparative collections are as follows:

	1939	1940
Tax collected	£32839	£29983
Tax payers	14777	13492

In December the clerk of Lusungo was imprisoned on a charge of theft. He had been "borrowing" tax money from 22 men who received no tickets from him. He offered no defence.

The planting of native food crops has been normal. There is little fear of this district approaching famine conditions since the continual rain eliminates the necessity of the fixed and all too short planting season. Rungwe District has always exported considerable quantities of maize, though the reduction in the requirements of the Lupa area has somewhat reduced the output. The rice crop in the Lake shore fell far short of production in 1939. This drop was due primarily to overflooding of the rice fields. Only 275 tons passed through the market as compared with 568 tons in 1939. This was not such a serious mishap for the growers as might have been expected owing to the high prices prevailing in the market at Kyela which averaging 17½ cents per kilogram, rose on one occasion to 19 cents. These prices are far too high to allow of export to the Central line and to compete economically with the rice producing areas of the Lake, Western and Eastern Provinces. If the crop is larger in future years, which is not an unduly optimistic assumption, it will be necessary for the growers to accept much smaller returns, since the local market where most of the rice is consumed, is not capable of any further expansion. The possibilities of a rice mill being erected and a market sought for the export of a better grade of rice through Nyasaland and Beira is under consideration.

As regards Rungwe Native Coffee it is feared that this at present is in a deplorable condition. Many plantations are riddled with disease, especially borer and Hemileia, others have been abandoned by their owners, while many are producing but meagre crops owing to neglect. This serious state of affairs is not due to any lack of propaganda nor yet of energetic action in the fields of Government, but has mainly been caused by an apathy and apparent lack of interest by the growers. It has now been decided to inaugurate a strenuous campaign to eradicate disease, each area being tackled systematically. A start has now been made in the worst area. The whole position has been particularly explained to the chiefs and others, who have been informed that the whole of the coffee industry is in such jeopardy that unless the growers realize the seriousness of the position and act promptly on the advice and orders given to them, Government may have shortly to consider abandoning native coffee growing in Rungwe.

It may be that much of the set back is due not only to bad cultivation and the past lack of control of disease, but also to the adverse soil conditions obtaining in many parts of the district. It is hoped to obtain expert advice on this matter during 1941.

Comparative figures relating to coffee sold in the markets are as follows:

	1938	1939	1940 (in tons)
Parchment	?	50	22
Hulled	?	7	26
Total	84	57	48

On the whole the proportion of coffee rejected at the markets, generally, owing to excessive moisture or antestia, was not so great as in 1939, though much better results could be obtained if the owners paid a little more heed to continual advice.

The large proportion of hulled coffee this year is due to the fact that very fortunate prices were obtained locally for this, and consequently many felt that a bird in the hand was well worth two in the bush. The price paid by the merchants concerned was 42 cents per kilo, of this the growers received 37 cents the remaining five being levy and cess credited to the Rungwe Native Treasury No. 2 Account. This compares very favourably with the price they received for parchment coffee last year when the cash return to the native was cents–/43 per kilo of *parchment*.

This year the parchment coffee is being cured in Mbeya and exported to Nyasaland and Southern Rhodesia where connections have been established which may prove of great value in future years. The price is £ 30 per ton f.o.b. the Lake Steamer, which should give the grower a return of some 48 cents per kilo.

Another sphere of native agriculture in which considerable progress has been made during the year is that of the prevention of soil erosion. It is estimated that some 60% of the cultivation is now under control. This represents a considerable advance and the natives are now adopting the measures advocated with a greater readiness.

The Medical Officer reports that the Tribal Dispensaries are continuing to give efficient service to the community, of over 114,000 attendances at Government and Native Administration Dispensaries up to the end of November, 77,000 attendances were at Native Administration Dispensaries. They are somewhat hampered by a shortage of drugs, but it is evident that the standard of the dressers and of the dispensaries buildings is well above that of many districts. Besides the rebuilding of one dispensary at Malangali, a new Government hospital is being built at Kyela. This will be an excellent building with large male and female wards and with good furniture and equipment, and should prove a great asset to the large population in the vicinity. The medical school, the cost of which is shared by all the Districts in the Province, continues to make good progress.

The rinderpest campaign at the beginning of the year produced very strong opposition at the outset. This however was overcome and the people accepted the position philosophically but grudgingly. Much of local cattle proved extremely susceptible to virus injections which resulted in a 75% mortality, and so vaccine was then given instead. Mortality was light and compensation was paid in all cases of proved deaths due to vaccination. The anti rinderpest campaign of 1917/18 was clearly alive in the memories of the Wanyakyusa so that it was only by dint of careful and tactful preparation of the ground that active opposition was not encountered. Even now complaints about lack of milk as a result of vaccination are frequent!

In the field of Education the boarding school at Mpuguso, for which much needed additional buildings were erected, has remained the centre of educational activity in the District. The teaching here is up to standard, but it is doubtful whether discipline is as strict as is desirable. The boys, 70 of whom are boarders—30 day boys— are full of life and strong lusty children, but their energies have not always been sufficiently directed. Tukuyu Government School in the Township, now to be taken over by the Native Administration has done well. Three new Native Administration day schools at Ikolo, Masoko and Ikama have been started during the year. The demand for educational facilities by the Wanyakyusa is considerable and it is anticipated that further day schools may be opened in 1941. The teachers and school materials are provided by Government but fees are charged (and willingly paid) which are designed to cover the teachers salary.

The Moravian Mission School at Rungwe, has been reopened under Government auspices, as a primary school with standards I to VI. This Mission is seeking to establish further schools and its progressive policy will help to satisfy the local craving for education.

The Native Administration has maintained its forestry nurseries. There is no difficulty in distributing the seedlings for the people are becoming more conscious of the benefits of reafforestation. Many are already in difficulties to obtain building poles and firewood so that it is hoped that the nuclei of Native Administration plantations may be an ocular demonstration, encouraging the widespread planting of trees by individuals, which is greatly needed.

Within the district some 800 labourers are in employment on the tea estates and coffee plantations. There has been a plentiful supply of labour though one estate employs a number of Wakinga from Njombe and at another there have been periodical shortages. The remedy for any shortage is in the planters own hands for wages remain on a low level. Relations between employers and employees have been most harmonious; in fact complaints by either party are extremely rare.

Voluntary labour has always been available for Government work for which wages have remained constant. The flow of labour to the Lupa Goldfields has been steady though not on the same scale as in past years. It is estimated that some 8,000 men went to work there during the year for varying periods. Many of these youths not yet of taxable age. Though work was not so easy to obtain as it was before the war, those who had previous connections had no difficulty about this. The numbers of men going to the Lupa have probably increased recently owing to the military recruiting in Rungwe.

Several hundreds of men have obtained work on the Mbozi farms, while a few of the more adventurous spirits have travelled as far as the Copper belt, and even Johannesburg.

Although this is a report on Native affairs it is nevertheless a suitable occasion to pay tribute to the work of Mr. Hall, who was in charge of this district from June, 1938 until the end of October, 1940 and who by his patent energy and deep interest in Native affairs has earned the gratitude of the natives of Rungwe.

J. F. R. Hill
DISTRICT COMMISSIONER.

B. J. J. STUBBINGS, O.B.E.

Handing-Over Notes, Mafia Island and
Mbwera (Rufiji District), 1945

Stubbings was born in 1915 and was educated in South Africa and at Oxford where he was a Rhodes Scholar. He joined the Tanganyika service in 1939. After a typical career in the provincial administration, broken by brief war service in Madagascar, he was government representative on a Tanganyika coffee commission to the United States and Canada in 1955. He retired in 1962.

Mafia, the third largest island off the Tanganyika coast, was a sleepy remnant of Arab days. In these handing-over notes Stubbings gives a concise summary of the island's government, economy, and society for the guidance of his successor.

Mbwera, geographically a part of Rufiji District on the mainland, was at this time administered from Mafia. Stubbings's notes on Mbwera contain interesting sidelights on cooperation between district officers and on such homely problems as mosquitoes in the delta.

*Handing-Over Notes,
Mafia Island and Mbwera (Rufiji District),
1945*

. . . J. Young Esq., A.D.O.

Since you are already acquainted with Mafia, these notes only refer to items with which you are probably not familiar. It will also perhaps be useful to give a brief account of activities during the first 10 months of this year which may be of assistance to you in compiling your Annual Report. I would also refer you to my Annual Report for 1944 (File 1/13/143). I shall add separate notes on Mbwera (Rufiji) now administered from Mafia.

A. *Office & Staff.*

Menezes you know. I have found him very reliable and useful. Fred Masongelana is slow but pleasant. His typing inaccuracies are probably often due to my vile handwriting.

The revocation of Deceased Native Estate Ordinance has tended to reduce the number of deceased estates with which the Kadhi has to deal but he is still invaluable in all such matters.

Kadhi is not in any way concerned with Produce Control work and Bakari Saidi E.C.B. clerk, works in the Boma and not in Kadhi's office as formerly. He has the routine at his finger tips.

B. *Administration.*

(a) *General.* The establishment of an Advisory Council is such a recent innovation that it is too early to comment on it. I feel it has many possibilities and will discuss it with you, although there will be little to add to what is in the Files (1/18 and 1/19).

The cessation of hostilities has made very little difference to life in Mafia. The parades and junketings held in connection with VE and VJ were well attended but no one will really believe the war is over until food and clothes etc. are again in plentiful supply.

(b) *Native Affairs.* The Akida of Utende has developed most encouragingly this year and has reacted well to the increased responsibility of acting the Kadhi's place while the latter was on leave.

I am little disappointed in the Akida of Kirongwe this year, although he is well and truly established. The very troublesome people of Beleni seem to be getting him down at times, but I have refused to have anything to do with Baleni shauris until the people concerned have gone to the Akida first. They almost invariably appeal against his settlements or court decisions but I have almost equally invariably found that his settlements or court decisions are very sound. With sympathetic backing, he will do well I feel. His Clerk is intelligent and useful.

The Jumbes are unchanged since your time except at Kirongwe and Chemchem. Both new Jumbes are doing well, particularly Sheha Kasiba at Kirongwe who is most energetic—a bit talkative perhaps but gets things done. Ali Haji's successor at Chemchem is Mohamed Saidi, an Arab but chosen by the Africans.

The Native Courts have been moderately busy and there is little to report. There is one outstanding appeal set down for hearing by A. O. i/c on 20/11/45. The Kadhi will have several appeals from Kirongwe to hear on his return and you will probably have to ginger him up to get them heard soon.

N. A.'s have made Orders under Sec. 8 (f) N. A. Ord: creating certain areas "Protected Forest Areas". You and Burrows started this. See File for correspondence. Other Orders under Sec. 8 have not yet been reduced to writing and this should be done for record purposes. See File 3/4.

(c) *Closing of Mafia as an Administrative Station.* Should it be necessary to take this most regrettable and in my humble opinion, most reprehensible step, you will find in file 1/14 details of arrangements provisionally made in 1944 which may be of assistance. See also my letter 1/14/31 and P. C.'s reply thereto (C. 25/4) at Red 32.

(d) *Non Native Affairs.* I have nothing to add to 1944 report except the unique event in Mafia of an Arab offering his services as a casual labourer to help pay his tax and get food.

C. *Labour.*

Still in very short supply. A series of prosecutions against offenders for failing to complete Kipandes and leaving employment when in debt has I hope helped to instal a little discipline into labourers. Fairly stiff sentences were inflicted.

D. *Communications.*

The "Azania" has been most irregular. Mails by Dhow have been very regular for the past three months and have averaged at least one a week.

My suggestion for Motorboat and Lorry mail service via Kisiju (see File 7/1/147) has not been replied to yet.

A new sub-postmaster not fully trained has recently been posted here but seems all right. His Cash should probably be checked more frequently than usual. This is not a reflection on his honesty but on his inexperience.

No aircraft has landed. The Landing ground was recently swept by fire and grass-cutting is not necessary just yet.

The motor boat is running excellently and has been in constant use. It is overdue for hauling up to dry out and repainting. The new nahodha Mohamed is good, and with Yussuf can take the boat anywhere.

Little work has been done on roads, except cleaning and repairing of 2 bridges. Both Kirongwe and Utende roads are passable. The Customs road is complete. A ready supply of "Kifusi" for road building is available on the shore at the Customs, and bits of road in Kilindoni particularly opposite the Hospital are due for repair. Funds are available. Three footbridges between Chemchem and Kiegeani are being repaired. One is done and paid for. Jumbe of Kiegeani is responsible.

E. *Medical.*

See File 1/19 re Advisory Council's request for a dispensary at Kirongwe.

Materials for Water supply to the hospital are en route.

2 Fatal cases of C.S.M. in Kilindoni in September necessitated quarantine.

Additional accommodations for more lepers at Ngeza has been built and new cases are in residence. A banda for store and since issued dispensary there is being erected. The patients are due for an issue of clothes now, and blankets will probably be available from the Gaol if write-off already applied for, is approved. A.D.S.I. Hatibu is the authority on Ngeza affairs. Small pangas and hoes are being made for patients by local fundi. Adequate funds are available for lepers.

F. *Education.*

African Village School attendance still unsatisfactory. A drive now for small children to start school in January '46 is essential. Withdrawing one teacher may be necessary. I asked Bubb to discuss this with you in Dar es Salaam before you left and will also see him myself. A house for the second teacher is now being built, but will always come in useful any way.

G. *Missions.* Nil.

H. *Land.*

See 1944 report and relevant files as to the compulsory registration of conveyances of trees between natives. This was not being done before.

I will explain the "drill" evolved for avoiding any repetition of the Ali Rashid hanky-panky.

As to the future fate of Custodian Properties see Secret File S. 2/83 and 86.

A Trading Centre has been laid out at Kirongwe and most plots sold. See File 11/14.

Nothing has been done to clear up the general muddle in Mafia, although I trust I have not made it any worse at any rate. The only outstanding land affair is an application by Esmail Lalji to purchase a shamba from Hussein Rashid Alibhai. I will discuss this with you. The documents are in the Confidential cupboard.

I. *Kilindoni Minor Settlement.*

Moderately clean. The possibility of obtaining water borne sanitation should not be forgotten. See Files 16/10/321 & 323 and 4/9/38 and 41.

K. *Trade.*

Mafia Produce Dealers Association still functions adequately and handles all produce and also Khangas and Piece Goods. The local distribution of Piece Goods I have left almost entirely to the merchants themselves and have had very few complaints. I recommend you to have as little to do with it as possible. So long as the consumer gets the goods at a fair price, the merchants can sort themselves out.

Sail Cloth and Fishing Line Thread urgently required but E.C.B. says there is none of the former and hasn't replied about the latter. See File 28/10.

There are some 22 score U.K. Khangas to be distributed—a small number the distribution of which will be difficult. For method of distribution previously used see File 28/10 or ask Bakari Saidi.

Copra. Despite much talk, more writing and even more agitating I regret to say I seem to have achieved absolutely nothing towards improving the quality and marketing of Copra. See File 6/5. The price has been very good for the past 2 years and the Mafia price although not "fixed" is fairly related to the Dar es Salaam Controlled price of Shgs. 4/85 per frasila.

Cashew Nuts. There is speculative market this year offering good prices. I have asked Agriculture Dar es Salaam and Senagric Lindi to send weekly wires giving prices to enable me to see that a fair price is being paid locally. The merchants here have formed a "syndicate" for buying Cashew Nuts to enable them to handle larger quantities and dispose of the nuts in bulk. I have no objections providing the price paid to the purchaser is fair. It looks like being a good Cashew Nut season.

Price Control. Goods in shops are marked with prices but whether goods are sold at these prices is a different question. I have advised the public to come to me if in any doubt as to prices but no one has come.

For goods, not locally price fixed flat rate of 10% on the appropriate column Dar es Salaam price is allowed.

For price fixing Piece Goods see File 28/10/336.

Produce Control. Owing to bad crops in the Rufiji and an inexplicable default by Southern Province it has been impossible to obtain sufficient Paddy or Mtama in bulk to last till July 1946. Accordingly Mafia now has to rely on expensive and unpopular Maize Meal from Dar es Salaam—30 tons per month. A small balance is being built up to enable increased issues in January and thereafter when really required. The local distribution system has been working satisfactorily for nearly 2 years now. Bakari Saidi knows it all.

6 Tons Mtama from Rufiji is arriving as also 15 tons Mtama promised from Dar es Salaam. Possibly early in 1946 Lindi, but not Kilwa, may be able to supply more Mtama. I advise you to enquire from Susup, Lindi in January if he can help at all. There are adequate supplies of Beans and Njugumawe in stock for many months if issued carefully.

While food here is so short, Dhows are rationed for trip to Dar es Salaam only, with food, but fully rationed for Sugar. Dhows have ration cards, and get balance of rations in Dar es Salaam.

Sugar is more plentiful but more is always welcome. Local distribution already worked out, I or Bakari Saidi can explain this.

L. *Agriculture.*

It has been a poor year all round with too much rain at the

wrong times, consequently there was a poor paddy harvest. A Sweet potato drive resulted in increased cultivation but the harvest was most disappointing. Sweet potatoes should be planted at least twice per year—during rains and after the Paddy Harvest.

There is quite a lot of Muhogo in the ground and more should go in January, February.

Cleaning and breaking of ground for Paddy etc. is now in progress. It will require prodding along as usual.

There is Paddy available for seed with the Association, but some reserve Paddy must be kept for food. (Some 250 bags Paddy in all in stock)

Thirty bags Kundo have been reserved for seed, with the Association. It will be issued very shortly.

For Coconut Sanitation see page 7 of 1944 Annual report. I have not done as much in this connection as I had hoped, and it is too late now for Native shambas at any rate.

Game Ranger has agreed to send Game Scout to deal with Hippo in March, April, May if you ask him in good time. He also wants to try out Pig poisoning experiments in Mafia, probably Juani, if Vermin Control staff are available. See minute on File Cover 6/11.

Jerusalem Artichokes have been introduced and do well in Kilindoni garden. Tubers have been distributed to all Jumbes for trial. It would be worth while getting them established as a "Kitoweo" but not as a substitute for Muhogo or Sweet Potatoes. Some "Caroline Lee" Sweet Potato cuttings have been also distributed to Jumbes.

M. *Forestry*.

The "protected areas" have been demarcated with firebreaks except at Changarama. The Coastal strip is not included. An old man is engaged as watchman for Kilindoni areas and has also to keep firebreaks cleaned.

N. *Veterinary*.

A small outbreak of East Coast Fever at present in the Ngombeni herd. No export of cattle permitted until the area is free of disease. The Veterinary Officer Dar es Salaam should be consulted as to relaxation of these restrictions.

Repairs to fence of Dipping Tank completed.

No fresh meat has been available for many months.

O. *Tours.*

Safari in Mafia has been interfered with by Rufiji safaris, but a fair amount has been done.

P. *Revenue and Expenditure.*

Native Tax. Practically 100% collection has been made and estimate already reached. Tax come in very well 85% being collected by end of February. You should have no difficulty in beating or at least equalling this. All persons who have not already been exempted for old age should pay in 1946. The assessment rolls fairly complete as to new tax payers for 1946. My estimate for 1946 tax is all over-estimate as it was made before my barazas exempting old men and entering youngsters. There were many of the former but very few of the latter. The African population is undoubtedly dwindling.

Non Native Poll Tax. Your policy re Indians and Arabs successfully followed and tax came in all right, but some Arab prosecutions were necessary.

I will go through the Vote Book with you. I am afraid funds are rather short all round at this time of the year.

Q. *Public Works.*

Works completed

(1) Police Lock Up.
(2) Police Latrines.
(3) Temporary repairs to Post Office Roof. See File 16/2/274 & 276.
(4) School ceiling.
(5) Mosquito proofing A. O.'s quarters.
(6) Customs Jetty and Sea Wall repaired.
(7) Utende Baraza-floor of beaten lime and walls with seats built.
(8) Rest House i.e. Menezes present quarters. Kitchen rebuilt.

Works in hand

(1) Second teacher's house, nearing completion.

Works to be completed if possible before end 1945

    (1) Collection of Makuti and Boriti for Kirongwe Market. Funds asked for in 1946.

    (2) Repairs to floor of Gaol if cement already ordered comes.

    (3) Water supply to Hospital and A.O.'s quarters. I will give you further details.

Works in 1946   See Estimates File for projected works.

P.W.D. Dar es Salaam have lent me one Mason, One Carpenter-Overseer, One Carpenter and One Carpenter's Mate who are to return to Dar es Salaam on completion of this year's works. They are paid from our Funds here, are expensive but very useful. P.W.D. have been *most* helpful and cooperative.

A young mason, trained by P.W.D. Mason is shaping well, and is worth retaining permanently if possible.

I have asked for provision of Shgs. 60/– p.m. in Station Hands Vote in 1946 for employment of a Full-Time Carpenter, Omari Mzee employed at present by Utete Native Treasury at Utete is a likely candidate as he is a native of Mafia.

R. *Meteorological.*

See Rainfall returns. I have advised Weather Dar es Salaam it will be necessary to close the stations at Kiegeani and Kirongwe as the present staff seem unable to cope with this simple job of recording daily rain fall and I have not time to supervise.

S. *Judicial.*

My court has been busier than I like. Depositions of 2 Preliminary Inquiries, one for Murder, and one for attempted Murder have recently forwarded to High Court. The 5 accused for Murder and 1 for attempted Murder are on remand in Goal here.

I'm afraid I have left you with 4 Civil cases set down for December (*before* I heard of my leave!!)

T. *Miscellaneous.*

    (1) *Police.* After a lot of trouble with police earlier there is

now a good crowd here under Cpl. Ziota who unfortunately wants to retire. There are now only 6 details here including 1 at Kirongwe which I have found quite adequate.

(2) *Crime.* The usual petty theft, but less house-breaking probably because the principal exponent, Mzee Barakala, is "inside" once again.

September was a bad month and included a Murder, an attempted Murder, and a Grievous Harm.

This is the "Uraka" season and there is the usual illicit brewing and consequent brawling. Native Authorities and Police have been instructed to look out for this.

(3) *Gaol.* 4/G/W Ramadhani in charge is very good and reliable. The other warders are fair. It will be necessary to import more convicts from Dar es Salaam immediately if you approve of this scheme, or to increase the Gaol population from local resources if essential services are to be maintained.

(4) *Flotsam & Jetsam.* One mine successfully dealt with at Juani. There is some salvage rubber in the Customs to be sent to Smith Mackenzie & Co. Ltd. who are now Dar es Salaam agents for Rubber.

(5) *Tembo Club.* Hours 12 to 8 P.M. reinstated. I hope funds will be provided in 1946 to put up a really good building.

(6) *Dhows etc.* See File 9/12/152 et seq for correspondence re Life Jackets. After some prosecutions, all large dhows i.e. those going to Dar es Salaam are now provided with life jackets. The small fishing boats are not provided yet, nor will they be unless prosecuted, which takes time which I have not been able to spare. In any case life jackets are still ridiculously expensive.

The restriction on Dhow movements by night has been lifted.

(7) *The Grass Fires (Control).* Ord. 1943. been applied to Mafia. This can be invoked when non-natives are involved. Native cases can be dealt with in Native Courts under orders made in connection with Coconut Sanitation (See 1944 report)

(8) *Deceased Estates.* There are some outstanding matters I'm afraid. I shall discuss these with you.

(9) *Visitors.* H. M. Minesweeper "Hatsuse"
        A. H. Savile, Senior Agricultural Officer
        A. G. de Villiers (Police)
        W. South (Police)
        H. J. Powell (Posts & Telegraphs)
        J. R. H. Dashwood (D.C. Utete)
        J. R. H. Hewlett (Game)
        Commissioner of Prison.

Mbwera

. . . [T]he part of the Rufiji Delta under the *Mtawala* of Mbwera which I will show you on the map, is now administered from Mafia, although still part of the Rufiji district—a rather difficult arrangement in many ways, which nevertheless seems to have worked moderately well.

The history of this arrangement you will find in file PF. 18 at Red 74 and 75 being D.C. Utete No. 11/11/113 of 30th April, 1945 and P. C.'s wire PF. 471/68. I have opened a Miscellaneous Rufiji Affairs file No. 1/18 where at Red 124 you will see from P.C.'s No. 6/5 of 5/10/45 that the Mbwera arrangement is to continue at present. I recommend a brief perusal of the file to give you an idea of the sort of things with which I have been dealing in Mbwera. I have arranged with D.C. Utete to have the minimum possible dealings with Cash and Licences etc. which are done from Utete.

The outstanding items for this year in Mbwera are:

(a) Native Tax Collection. 92% has been collected but some 218 taxes are still unpaid. Tax collection there is not easy and for the balance, a safari by yourself as soon as possible, at all events before 15th December when Rufiji Tax collections close at Utete Boma, will be necessary. A few prosecutions will probably be essential.

(b) Completion of the fish market at Mbwera. I will discuss this with you. Also collection of stone for next year's buildings at Mbwera.

(c) Some small shauris which I will explain personally.

(d) Seeing that the Cotton is picked properly and sold. I recommend you to visit Msomeni to discuss Cotton buying with Dourado, the Goan Manager at the Ginnery. He is very helpful and obliging.

(e) Getting Paddy shambas cleaned up ready for planting.

In general the Mbwera people are not very attractive and are as idle as you will allow them to be, except at Usimbe where they are quite industrious. Mbwera itself is a hive of "fitina" and idle corner boys living on theft largely, one must assume. The Mtawala has improved recently and is beginning to get a hold again, but he needs a lot of jogging along, and is rather too keen on "huruma" where some straightforward discipline is required. However I feel that the majority of people there do appreciate such small increase in attention as it has been possible to give them in recent months.

There is incidentally absolutely no reason why at least 75% of Mbwera Tax should not be collected before March each year. They are rich in Coconuts, Cotton, to a lesser extent Paddy, and Ghaui provides plenty of work, although his system of giving advances is rapidly ruining the district and gives endless trouble to the Native Court.

The Native Court unless carefully watched, will get badly into arrears in Civil Cases. Considerable arrears have been cleared up this year. The litigants are principally at fault and I have instructed the Mtawala that dilatory litigants should receive no sympathy at all.

The Mbwera branch of the African Association has recently been opened. Some fears of its possibly subversive nature were at first entertained but I have seen or heard of nothing to support this theory.

Price Control at Mbwera needs watching. Two successful prosecutions have been made, and things are probably improved.

In general you will find it difficult to give the close personal attention to Mbwera that you can give to Mafia owing to the way the area is broken up by rivers and swamps.

A final, personal warning. The mosquitoes at Mbwera are wicked and I recommend a "dining net" as well as an ordinary net and keeping well covered with slacks and long sleeves, between the hours of 4 P.M. and 10 A.M.

B. J. J. Stubbings,
A. D. O.

SOURCES

Published works and other printed materials have been referred to in footnotes. Bibliographies on Tanganyika may be found in the following: *The Handbook of Tanganyika Territory*, ed. G. F. Sayers, London, 1930; *Handbook of Tanganyika*, ed. J. P. Moffett, Dar es Salaam, 1958; *Tanganyika: A Review of Its Resources and Their Development*, ed. J. F. R. Hill and J. P. Moffett, Dar es Salaam, 1955; Margaret L. Bates, "Tanganyika under British Administration, 1920–1955," doctoral thesis, Oxford University, 1957; *History of East Africa*, 2 vols., Oxford, 1963, 1965; J. Clagett Taylor, *The Political Development of Tanganyika*, Stanford, 1963; Ralph Austen, *Northwest Tanzania under German and British Rule*, New Haven, 1968; *Tanganyika Notes and Records*, 1936ff.

I. *National Archives of Tanzania*

Arusha, Headquarters Northern Province, 1924–1954
    Division of the territory into provinces
    Amalgamation of tribal areas
    Tour reports
    Opening of Loliondo station
    German settlers
    Resident magistrates
    Land development
    Land alienation
    Settlers, general

Arusha District, 1926–1956
    Liwali and staff
    Native authority, general
    Financial correspondence
    African instructors
    Estimates
Arusha District Book (all districts, Northern Province)

Bagamoyo District
    Administrative policy
    TANU
    Safari notes
    Township authority, minutes
Bagamoyo District Book

Bukoba District, 1918–1955
    District Court records
    Liwali and headmen

Dodoma District, 1926–1958
    Handing-over notes
    TANU
    Native court warrants
    Famine relief
    African civil service
    Vote Book
    Native treasuries, Central Province
    Labor
    Agricultural policy
    Abolition of tribute
    Reform of native authority

Iringa District, 1926–1956
    Chief Adam Sapi
    Native affairs
    District Officers' safari reports
    Policy and instructions
Papers from Iringa District Headquarters. List of District Officers
    in charge, 1926–1958. Tribal government history, precolonial
    and British. (Provided by Professor Norman N. Miller)

Kilosa District, 1935–1958
    Annual reports
    Handing-over notes

Kisarawe District, 1942–1952
    Monthly reports to Provincial Commissioner
    Reorganization, Kisarawe Uzaramo District
Kisarawe District Book, District Headquarters

Lindi Provincial Headquarters, 1929–1952
 Provincial administration, policy and instructions
 League of Nations and United Nations
 Staff: Regulations

Lushoto District, 1927–1954
 Tour notes, Tanga, Handeni, Lushoto

Mbeya District, 1930–1951
 Administrative circulars
 Africanization and training

Monduli Boma, 1926–1953
 Masai District reorganization
 Native authority
 Laibon and Ilaigwanak

Morongoro District and Eastern Province Headquarters, 1925–1952
 Native authorities
 Labor contracts
 District Officers' touring notes
 Markets
 Roads
 Native courts
 Governor's visits

Moshi District, 1918–1950
 Native authorities
 Appeals to District Officer's Court
 Water disputes, German East Africa
 Chiefs

Mtwara District (Mikindani) 1926–1955
 Policy
 Native languages
 Training of natives
 Native revolt of 1905
 Sociological investigations

Mwanza District and Provincial Headquarters, 1922–1958
 General correspondence
 Ecclesiastical policy and White Fathers Mission

Native affairs
Land registration
Petitions
Witchcraft
Medical reports
Whipping, native courts
Township authority

Mwanza District Book, Lake Province Headquarters, including material on all East Lake Districts

Njombe District, 1925–1936
Safari reports
Tribal notes

Pangani District, 1921–1952
Liwali
Tribal messengers
Settlement of Arab Estates

Rungwe District (Tukuyu), 1927–1959
Native administration
Federation of Chiefs
Witchcraft

Papers from Rungwe District Headquarters. List of District Officers in charge 1916–1961. Historical notes before British occupation. Traditional government, labor, education. (Provided by Professor Norman N. Miller)

Singida District, 1920–1957
Asiatic staff
Native affairs
Subchiefs and Jumbes
Reclamation schemes

Tabora District, 1929–1959
Chiefs
District Officers' correspondence
Safari reports

Tanga District, 1925–1955
African administration
Land files

Papers of the National Museum, Dar es Salaam. Extracts from district books (Mbeya, Njombe, Musoma, Rungwe) and ethnographic notes from various districts.

Secretariat Files. Including correspondence between Secretariat and members of the provincial administration and the technical and professional services, circulars, minutes of provincial commissioners' conferences and special committees, native authority districts, ordinances, correspondence with the United Kingdom, annual reports.

II. *Colonial Records Project*, Oxford University (general administrative papers unless otherwise noted)

F. J. E. Bagshawe: Diaries, tribal studies, annual reports, missions, Handing-over reports
E. C. Baker: Tribal histories, commonplace books
W. S. G. Barnes: Letterbook, safari diaries, reports
A. K. Bate
H. C. Baxter: Personal papers and scholarly articles
C. F. C. V. Cadiz
Sir Reginald Coupland: Travel diaries, East Africa, 1928
B. J. Dudbridge: Tribal papers
J. E. S. Griffiths: Diaries, safari notes
F. C. Hallier
J. F. R. Hill
E. H. A. Leakey
E. K. Lumley: Diary
H. H. McCleery
G. St. J. Orde Browne: Papers on native labor
W. F. Page
J. Rooke Johnston: Reports, diary
B. W. Savory
G. A. Tomlinson: Safari diary, letters, and other papers
W. B. Tripe: Letters
L. A. W. Vickers-Haviland

C. Whybrow: Diaries, journal and reports, Education Service
A. W. Wyatt
Tanganyika District Books, microfilmed

III. *Private Papers*

Correspondence of Sir Donald Cameron (with Lord Lugard and others), privately held.
J. F. R. Hill: Notes on administrative service in Tanganyika
F. Longland: Notes on administrative service in Tanganyika
W. F. Page: Notes on administrative service in Tanganyika
J. Rooke Johnston: Unpublished manuscript, dealing mainly with Kigoma, 1930s, 28 pp.
B. W. Savory: Notes on administrative service in Tanganyika
J. J. Tawney: Unpublished manuscript, describing service in Tanganyika, 1930ff., 44 pp.
J. J. Tawney: Tape recorded memoire of service in Kasulu District, 1940s

INDEX

Abdieli, Chief of Machame, 71–72
Adultery, charges of, 115, 120
Africa: English attitudes toward, 8; Europeans in, 4, 9
African Association, 59–60, 61, 137
Agriculture, 8, 18, 25, 37, 38; and colonial administration, 41, 65; on Mafia Island, 131–32; native African, 79, 81, 96, 99, 105, 114, 121–23
Alcoholism, 27
Alimasi, Hamida, 49
Amani, research station at, 14
Angoni, 30, 46, 51, 79, 96, 111
Anthropology, 58n; DOs and, 34
Appeal, courts of, 85–86, 120
Arabs in East Africa, 13, 70, 79, 104, 115, 126, 127, 128, 133
Arson, 86
Arusha District, 13n, 15n, 25, 33, 34n, 36n, 41n, 43n, 45n, 56n, 58n, 61, 64, 67n, 139; tribesmen, 67, 68n
Austen, Ralph, 59n, 139

Bagamoyo District, 12, 14, 23n, 32n, 34n, 48, 60, 64n, 107, 140
Bagenal, C. J., 14
Bagshawe, F. J. E., 8, 12, 18–19, 23n, 27, 42
Baker, E. C. "Jumbe," 28n
Baleni, 127
Bampfylde, F. W., 15, 60n
Banana trees, 98
Barakala, Mzee, 135
Barnabus, son of Ngalami, 72
Barnes, W. S. G., vii, 10–11, 17
Basingo clan, 91
Baxter, H. C., vii, 25n, 31n, 34n
Beans: cultivation of, 99, 131; in safari food ration, 95, 97, 98, 100, 103, 113
Beekeeping, 96, 99, 102, 104, 106, 109
Beeswax, trade in, 98, 100, 104, 109, 110, 111
Beira, 122

Belgium, 81; Belgian rule in Congo, 8, 9, 10, 14; rule in Tanganyika, 111, 112
Bell, G. F., 19n
Bena tribesmen, 50, 82
Berliner Mission, Matema, 82
Berne, J. L., 42, 48n
Biharamulo District, 89
Bilali, Headman, 104
Birds, 104, 110, 112
Birth rates, 97, 106, 107
Boer Revolt, 9
Bombwe, 113, 114, 115
Bone, R., vii, 33, 61, 62
Boundaries, 16–17, 76–78, 96, 103, 104; disputes over, 119
Bride price, 97n, 107
Bridges, 120, 129
Britain, 3, 4; Colonial Office, 19, 30, 43; expatriates from, 9; rule in Tanganyika, 5–7, 10–14, 20–21, 36, 45, 65–66; toured by Tanganyikan chiefs, 51. See also Colonial administration
Bronchitis, 97, 102, 114
Buffalo, 104, 105, 113
Buganda, 58
Bugwe, 103, 108, 110
Buholoholo, 109
Building construction, 120, 124, 129, 133–34, 135
Bujunja, Headman, 102, 103
Bukoba District, xi, 45n, 53n, 56, 62, 140
Bukwama, 78
Bulamata, 103
Bulimba, 105
Bulongwa, 75, 82
Bundali, 117, 119
Bureaucracy, colonial, 63, 67; DOs and, 19, 41–43, 65, 66
Burial practices, 24
Burton, Sir Richard, 8
Bus fares, 60
Bushamba, 103, 108, 110
Byatt, Sir Horace, 20n, 46, 52